Spurgeon's Sermons on the Resurrection of Christ

Books by C. H. Spurgeon

A Classic Bible Study Library for Today
Commenting and Commentaries
Day by Day with C. H. Spurgeon (compiled by Al Bryant)
The Treasury of David (edited by David Otis Fuller)
Spurgeon's Sermon Illustrations
Spurgeon's Sermon Notes
Spurgeon's Sermons on the Cross of Christ
Spurgeon's Sermons on Old Testament Men • Book One
Spurgeon's Sermons on Old Testament Women • Book One
Spurgeon's Sermons on Prayer
Spurgeon's Sermons on the Resurrection of Christ
Spurgeon's Sermons on Soul-Winning

C.H. Spurgeon Sermon Series

Spurgeon's Sermons on the Resurrection of Christ

CHARLES HADDON SPURGEON

Kregel Publications
Grand Rapids, MI 49501

Spurgeon's Sermons on the Resurrection of Christ by Charles H. Spurgeon.

Published in 1993 by Kregel Publications, a division of Kregel, Inc., P.O. Box 2607, Grand Rapids, MI 49501.

Cover and book design: Alan G. Hartman

Library of Congress Cataloging-in-Publication Data

Spurgeon, C. H. (Charles Haddon), 1834-1892.
[Sermons on the resurrection of Christ]
Spurgeon's Sermons on the Resurrection of Christ / by Charles H. Spurgeon.
p. cm.
1. Jesus Christ—Resurrection—Sermons.
2. Sermons, English. I. Title.
BT481.S74 1993 232'.5—dc20 93-13812
CIP

ISBN 0-8254-3686-9 (pbk.)

1 2 3 4 5 printing / year 97 96 95 94 93

Printed in the United States of America

Contents

Foreword

The idea of resurrection is a distinctly New Testament concept. There was little teaching about resurrection in the Old Testament, for there people were thought to enter Sheol, the place of the departed, when they died. Jesus' own teaching about resurrection was largely concerned with predictions that He Himself would rise from the dead. Thus it is the witness of the New Testament that the Resurrection of Jesus is the pivotal point of Christian theology—and it is the *fact* of the Resurrection and its consequences that underlies the sermons selected for this anthology. Included are several sermons dealing with events which would not have happened if Jesus had not risen from the dead (i.e., the Ascension).

In his book, *The Four Faces of Jesus* (Kregel, 1993), Dr. Leslie B. Flynn deals with the pivotal place of the Resurrection in relationship to our faith:

> Some who speak of the resurrection do not mean that He rose bodily. Engaging in mental gymnastics, they claim it was His influence that came out of the grave, not His body. Hearing a pastor so refer to the resurrection, a congregation may not realize that he does not believe in a literal resurrection. To such a pastor, Jesus' body never emerged from the tomb—it was His spirit that rose.
>
> To deny that the body of Christ rose, while at the same time affirming His resurrection, sounds like double-talk and smacks of intellectual dishonesty.

He goes on to point out that:

> Such dialogue is theological equivocation. The four Gospels plainly assert Jesus' literal resurrection. Except for the graveclothes, the tomb was empty and His body risen. To His frightened disciples He showed Himself alive with many infallible proofs.

The New Testament records eleven appearance of the risen Christ which occurred before His ascension:

- To *Mary*, who reached the tomb after Peter and John left it (Mark 16:9; John 20:11-18);

- To the *women* after leaving the tomb (Matt. 28:9,10);
- To *Peter* (Luke 24:34; 1 Cor. 15:5);
- To the *two* on the Emmaus road (Luke 24:13-35);
- To the *ten* disciples and others—minus Thomas (Luke 24:33-45; John 20:19-23);
- To the *eleven*, including Thomas (John 20:24-29);
- To *several disciples* fishing on Galilee (John 21);
- To the *disciples* on a Galilean mount (Matt. 28:16-20);
- To *five hundred brethren* at once (1 Cor. 15:6);
- To *James* (1 Cor. 15:7);
- To the *disciples* at the Ascension (Mark 16:19; Luke 24:50-52; Acts 1:9-11).

The sermons selected for this anthology are taken from *The Metropolitan Tabernacle Pulpit*, the massive 63-volume set published over a period of many years. It is the compiler's prayer that this collection of sermons will bless your private as well as your public ministry of the Word.

AL BRYANT

Grand Rapids, Michigan
1993

1

*The Resurrection of Our Lord Jesus**

Remember that Jesus Christ of the seed of David was raised from the dead according to my gospel (2 Timothy 2:8).

From long sickness my mind is scarcely equal to the work before me. Certainly, if I had ever sought after brilliance of thought or language, I should have failed today, for I am almost at the lowest stage of incapacity. I have only been comforted in the thought of preaching to you by the reflection that it is the doctrine itself which God blesses, and not the way in which it may be spoken; for if God had made the power to depend upon the speaker and his style, He would have chosen that the Resurrection, grandest of all truths, should have been proclaimed by angels rather than by men. Yet He set aside the seraph for the humbler creature. After angels had spoken a word or two to the women their testimony ceased.

The most prominent testimony to the resurrection of the Lord was at the first that of holy women, and afterwards that of each one of the guileless men and women who made up the five hundred or more whose privilege it was to have actually seen the risen Savior, and who therefore could bear witness to what they had seen, though they may have been quite unable to describe with eloquence what they had beheld.

Upon our Lord's rising I having nothing to say, and God's ministers have nothing to say, beyond bearing witness to the fact that Jesus Christ of the seed of David was raised from the dead. Put it in poetry, tell it out in sublime Miltonic verse, it will come to no more; tell it out in monosyllables, and write it so that little children may read it in their first spelling-books, and it will come to nothing less. "The Lord is risen indeed"

---

* This sermon is taken from *The Metropolitan Tabernacle Pulpit* and was preached on Sunday morning, April 9, 1882.

is the sum and substance of our witness when we speak of our risen Redeemer. If we do but know the truth of this resurrection, and feel the power of it, our mode of utterance is of secondary consequence; for the Holy Spirit will bear witness to the truth, and cause it to produce fruit in the minds of our hearers.

Our present text is found in Paul's second letter to Timothy. The venerable minister is anxious about the young man who has preached with remarkable success, and whom he regards in some respects as his successor. The old man is about to put off his tabernacle, and he is concerned that his son in the gospel should preach the same truth as his father has preached, and should by no means adulterate the gospel. A tendency showed itself in Timothy's day, and the same tendency exists at this very hour, to try to get away from the simple matters of fact upon which our religion is built, to something more philosophical and hard to be understood. The word which the common people heard gladly is not fine enough for cultured sages, so they must needs surround it with a mist of human thought and speculation. Three or four plain facts constitute the gospel, even as Paul puts it in the fifteenth chapter of his first epistle to the Corinthians: "For I delivered unto you first of all that which I also received, how that Christ died for our sins according to the Scriptures; and that he was buried, and that he rose again the third day according to the Scriptures."

Upon the incarnation, life, death and resurrection of Jesus our salvation hinges. He who believes these truths aright has believed the gospel, and believing the gospel he shall without doubt find eternal salvation therein. But men want novelties; they cannot endure that the trumpet should give forth the same certain sound, they crave some fresh fantasia every day. "*The gospel with variations*" is the music for them. Intellect is progressive, they say; they must, therefore, march ahead of their forefathers. Incarnate Deity, a holy life, an atoning death, and a literal resurrection—having heard these things now for nearly nineteen centuries they are just a little stale, and the cultivated mind hungers for a change from the old-fashioned manna. Even in Paul's day this tendency was manifest, and so they sought to regard facts as mysteries or parables, and they labored to find a spiritual meaning in them till they went so far as to deny them as actual facts.

Seeking a recondite meaning, they overlooked the fact itself, losing the substance in a foolish preference for the shadow. While God set before them glorious events which fill heaven with amazement they showed their foolish wisdom by accepting the plain historical facts as myths to be interpreted or riddles to be solved. He who believed as a little child was pushed aside as a fool that the disputer and the scribe might come in to mystify simplicity, and hide the light of truth. Hence there had arisen a certain Hymenaeus and Philetus, "who concerning the truth have erred, saying that the resurrection is past already; and overthrow the faith of some" (2 Tim. 2:18). They spirited away the resurrection; they made it to mean something very deep and mystical, and in the process they took away the actual resurrection altogether.

Among men there is still a craving after new meanings, refinements upon old doctrines, and spiritualizations of literal facts. They tear out the bowels of the truth, and give us the carcass stuffed with hypotheses, speculations, and larger hopes. The golden shields of Solomon are taken away, and shields of brass are hung up in their stead: will they not answer every purpose, and is not the metal more in favor with the age? It may be so, but we never admired Rehoboam, and we are old-fashioned enough to prefer the original shields of gold. The apostle Paul was very anxious that Timothy at least should stand firm to the old witness, and should understand in their plain meaning his testimonies to the fact that Jesus Christ of the seed of David rose again from the dead.

Within the compass of this verse several facts are recorded: and, first, there is here the great truth that *Jesus, the Son of the Highest, was anointed of God*; the apostle calls Him "Jesus *Christ*" that is, the anointed one, the Messiah, the sent of God. He calls Him also "*Jesus*," which signifies a Savior, and it is a grand truth that He who was born of Mary, He who was laid in the manger at Bethlehem, He who loved and lived and died for us, is the ordained and anointed Savior of men. We have not a moment's doubt about the mission, office, and design of our Lord Jesus; in fact, we hang our soul's salvation upon His being anointed of the Lord to be the Savior of men.

This *Jesus Christ was really and truly man*; for Paul says He was "*of the seed of David*." True He was divine, and His birth was not after the ordinary manner of men, but still He was in all respects partaker of our human nature, and came of the stock of David. This also we do believe. We are not among those who spiritualize the incarnation, and suppose that God was here as a phantom, or that the whole story is but an instructive legend. Nay, in very flesh and blood did the Son of God abide among men: bone of our bone and flesh of our flesh was He in the days of His sojourn here below. We know and believe that Jesus Christ has come in the flesh. We love the incarnate God, and in Him we fix our trust.

It is implied, too, in the text that *Jesus died*; for He could not be raised from the dead if He had not first gone down among the dead, and been one of them. Yes, Jesus died: the crucifixion was no delusion, the piercing of His side with a spear was most clear and evident proof that He was dead: His heart was pierced, and the blood and water flowed therefrom. As a dead man He was taken down from the cross and carried by gentle hands, and laid in Joseph's virgin tomb. I think I see that pale corpse, white as a lily. Mark how it is stained with the blood of His five wounds, which make

Him red as the rose. See how the holy women tenderly wrap Him in fine linen with sweet spices, and leave Him to spend His sabbath all alone in the rock-hewn sepulcher. No man in this world was ever more surely dead than He. "He made His grave with the wicked and with the rich in His death" (Isa. 53:9). As dead they laid Him in the place of the dead, with napkin and grave-clothes, and habiliments fit for a grave: then they rolled the great stone at the grave's mouth and left Him, knowing that He was dead.

Then comes the grand truth, that as soon as ever the third sun commenced His shining circuit *Jesus rose again.* His body had not decayed, for it was not possible for that holy thing to see corruption; but still it had been dead; and by the power of God—by His own power, by the Father's power, by the power of the Spirit—for it is attributed to each of these in turn, before the sun had risen His dead body was quickened. The silent heart began again to beat, and through the stagnant canals of the veins the life-flood began to circulate. The soul of the Redeemer again took possession of the body, and it lived once more. There He was within the sepulcher, as truly living as to all parts of Him as He had ever been. He literally and truly, in a material body, came forth from the tomb to live among men till the hour of His ascension into heaven. This is the truth which is still to be taught, refine it who may, spiritualize it who dare. This is the historical fact which the apostles witnessed; this is the truth for which the confessors bled and died. This is the doctrine which is the key-stone of the arch of Christianity, and they that hold it not have cast aside the essential truth of God. How can they hope for salvation for their souls if they do not believe that "the Lord is risen indeed"?

In this message I wish to do three things. First, let us *consider the bearings of the resurrection of Christ upon the great truths*; secondly, let us *consider the bearings of this fact upon the gospel*, for it has such bearings, according to the text—Jesus Christ of the seed of David was raised from the dead according to my gospel;" thirdly, let us *consider its bearings on ourselves*, which are all indicated in the word, "Remember."

Bearings of the Resurrection upon Other Great Truths

First, then, beloved, as God shall help us, let us consider the BEARINGS OF THE FACT THAT JESUS ROSE FROM THE DEAD.

It is clear at the outset that *the resurrection of our Lord was a tangible proof that there is another life.* Have you not quoted a great many times certain lines about "that undiscovered country from whose borne no traveler returns"? It is not so. There was once a traveler who said that "I go to prepare a place for you, and if I go away I will come again and receive you unto myself; that where I am there ye may be also." He said, "A little time and ye shall see me, and again a little time and ye shall not see me, and because I go the Father" (John 14:3, 19). Do you not remember these words of His? Our divine Lord went to the undiscovered country, and He returned. He said that at the third day He would be back again, and He was true to His word.

There is no doubt that there is another state for human life, for Jesus has been in it, and has come back from it. We have no doubt as to a future existence, for Jesus existed after death. We have no doubt as to a paradise of future bliss, for Jesus went to it and returned. Though He has left us again, yet that coming back to tarry with us forty days has given us a sure pledge that He will return a second time when the hour is due, and then will be with us for a thousand years, and reign on earth amongst His ancients gloriously. His return from among the dead is a pledge to us of existence after death, and we rejoice in it.

His resurrection is also a pledge that the body will surely live again and rise to a superior condition; for the body of our blessed Master was no phantom after death any more than before. "Handle me, and see."

O wondrous proof! He said, "Handle me, and see"; and then to Thomas, "Reach hither thy finger, and behold my hands; and reach hither thy hand, and thrust it into my side" (John 20:27). What deception is possible here? The risen Jesus was no mere spirit. He promptly cried, "A spirit hath not flesh and bones, as ye see me have." "Bring me," said He, "something to eat"; and as if to show how real His body was, though He did not need to eat, yet He did eat, and a piece of a broiled fish and of an honeycomb were proofs of the reality of the act.

Now, the body of our Lord in its risen state did not exhibit the whole of His glorification; for otherwise we should have seen John falling at His feet as dead, and we should have seen all His disciples overcome with the glory of the vision; but, still, in a great measure, we may call the forty days' sojourn—"The life of Jesus in His glory upon earth." He was no longer despised and rejected of men; but a glory surrounded Him.

It is evident that the raised body passed from place to place in a single moment, that it appeared and vanished at will, and was superior to the laws of matter. The risen body was incapable of pain, of hunger, thirst, and weariness during the time in which it remained here below—fit representative of the bulk of which it was the first-fruits. Of our body also it shall be said ere long, "It was sown in weakness, it is raised in power: it was sown in dishonor, it is raised in glory" (1 Cor. 15:43, 44). Let us, then, as we think of the risen Christ, rest quite sure of a future life, and quite sure that our body will exist in it in a glorified condition.

I do not know whether you are ever troubled with doubts in connection with the world to come as to whether it can be true that we shall live eternally. Here is the respect which makes death so terrible to doubters; for while they have realized the grave, they have not realized the life beyond it. Now, the best help to that realization is a firm grip of the fact that Jesus died and Jesus rose again. This fact is proved better than any other event in history; the witness to it is far stronger than to anything else that is written either in profane or sacred records. The rising of our Lord Jesus Christ being certain, you may rest assured of the existence of another world. That is the first bearing of this great truth.

Secondly, *Christ's rising from the dead was the seal to all His claims.* It was true, then, that He was sent of God, for God raised Him from the dead in confirmation of His mission. He had said Himself, "Destroy this body, and in three days I will raise it up." Lo, there He is: the temple of His body is rebuilt! He had even given this as a sign, that as Jonah was three days and three nights in the whale's belly, so should the Son of man be three days and three nights in the heart of the earth, and should then come forth to life again. Behold His own appointed sign fulfilled! Before men's eye the seal is manifest! Suppose Christ had never risen. You and I might have believed in the truth of a certain mission which God had given Him; but we could never have believed in the truth of such a commission as He claimed to have received—a commission to be our Redeemer from death and hell. How could He be our ransom from the grave if He had himself remained under the dominion of death?

Dear friends, the rising of Christ from the dead proved that this man was innocent of every sin. He could not be holden by the bands of death, for there was no sin to make those bands fast. Corruption could not touch His pure body, for no original sin had defiled the Holy One. Death could not keep Him a continual prisoner, because He had not actually come under sin; and though He took sin of ours, and bore it by imputation, and therefore died, yet He had no fault of His own, and must, therefore, be set free when His imputed load had been removed.

Moreover, Christ's rising from the dead proved His claim to Deity. We are told in another place that He was proved to be the Son of God with power by the resurrection from the dead. He raised Himself by His own power, and though the Father and the Holy Spirit were cooperative with Him, and hence His resurrection is ascribed to Them, yet it was because the Father had given Him to have life in Himself, that therefore He arose from the dead. O risen Savior, Your rising is the seal of Your work! We can have no doubt about You now that You have left the tomb. Prophet of Nazareth, You are indeed the Christ of God, for God has loosed the bands of death for You! Son of David,You are indeed the elect and precious One, for You ever live! Your resurrection life has set the sign-manual of heaven to all that You have said and done, and for this we bless and magnify Your name.

A third bearing of His resurrection is this, and it is a very grand one—*The resurrection of our Lord, according to the Scripture, was the acceptance of His sacrifice.* By the Lord Jesus Christ rising from the dead evidence was given that He had fully endured the penalty which was due to human guilt. "The soul that sinneth it shall die" (Ezek. 18:20)—that is the determination of the God of heaven. Jesus stands in the sinner's stead and dies: and when He has done *that* nothing more can be demanded of him, for he that is dead is free from the law. You take a man who has been guilty of a capital offense: he is condemned to be hanged, he is hanged by the neck till he is dead—what more has the law to do with him? It has done with him, for it has executed its sentence upon him; if he can be brought back to life again he is clear from the law; no writ that runs in Her Majesty's dominions can touch him—he has suffered the penalty. So when our Lord Jesus rose from the dead, after having died, He had fully paid the penalty that was due to justice for the sin of His people, and his new life was a life clear of penalty, free from liability. You and I are clear from the claims of the law because Jesus stood in our stead, and God will not exact payment both from us and from our Substitute: it were contrary to justice to sue both the Surety and those for whom He stood. And now, joy upon joy! the burden of liability which once did lie upon the Substitute is removed from Him also; seeing He has by the suffering of death vindicated justice and made satisfaction to the injured law. Now both the sinner and the Surety are free.

This is a great joy, a joy for which to make the golden harps ring out a loftier style of music. He who took our debt has now delivered himself from it by dying on the cross. His new life, now that He has risen from the dead, is a life free from legal claim, and it is the token to us that we whom He represented are free also. Listen! "Who shall lay anything to the charge of God's elect? It is God that justifieth. Who is he that condemneth? It is Christ that died, yea rather, that is risen again" (Rom. 8:33, 34).

It is a knockdown blow to fear when the apostle says that we cannot be condemned because Christ has died in our stead, but he puts a double force into it when he cries, "Yea rather, that is risen again." If Satan, therefore, shall come to any believer and say, "What about your sin?" tell him Jesus died for it, and your sin is put away. If he come a second time, and say to you, "What about your sin?" answer him, "Jesus lives, and His life is the assurance of our justification; for if our Surety had not paid the debt He would still be under the power of death."

Inasmuch as Jesus has discharged all our liabilities, and left not one farthing due to God's justice from one of His people, He lives and is clear, and we live in Him, and are clear also by virtue of our union with Him. Is not this a glorious doctrine, this doctrine of the resurrection, in its bearing upon the justification of the saints? The Lord Jesus gave Himself for our sins, but He rose again for our justification.

Bear with me while I notice, next, another bearing of this resurrection of Christ. *It was a guarantee of His people's resurrection.* There is a great truth that never is to be forgotten, namely, that Christ and His people are one just as Adam and all his seed are one. That which Adam did he did as a head for a body, and as our Lord Jesus and all believers are one, so that which Jesus did He did as a head for a body. We were crucified together with Christ, we were buried with Christ, and we are risen together with Him; yea, He has raised us up together and made us sit together in the heavenly places in Christ Jesus. He says, "Because I live ye shall live also."

If Christ be not raised from the dead your faith is vain, and our preaching is vain, and you are yet in your sins, and those who have fallen asleep in Christ have perished, and you will perish too; but if Christ has been raised from the dead then all His people must be raised also; it is a matter of gospel necessity. There is no logic more imperative than the argument drawn from union with Christ. God has made the saints one with Christ, and if Christ has risen all the saints must rise too. My soul takes firm hold on this and as she strengthens her grasp she loses all fear of death. Now we bear our dear ones to the cemetery and leave them each one in his narrow cell, calmly bidding him farewell and saying:

> So Jesus slept: God's dying Son
> Pass'd through the grave, and blest the bed;
> Rest here, dear saint, till from His throne
> The morning break, and pierce the shade.

It is not merely ours to know that our brethren are living in heaven, but also that their mortal parts are in divine custody, securely kept till the appointed hour when the body shall be reanimated, and the perfect man shall enjoy the adoption of God. We are sure that our dead men shall live; together with Christ's dead body they shall rise. No power can hold in durance the redeemed of the Lord. "Let my people go" shall be a command as much obeyed by death as once by the humbled Pharaoh who could not hold a single Israelite in bonds. The day of deliverance comes on apace.

> Break from His throne, illustrious morn!
> Attend, O earth, His sovereign word;
> Restore thy trust, a glorious form:
> He must ascend to meet his Lord.

Once more, *our Lord's rising from the dead is a fair picture of the new life which all believers already enjoy*. Beloved, though this body is still subject to bondage like the rest of the visible creation, according to the law stated in Scripture, "the body is dead because of sin," yet "the spirit is life because of righteousness." The regeneration which has taken place in those who believe has changed our spirit, and given to it eternal life, but it has not affected our body further than this, that it has made it to be the temple of the Holy Spirit, and thus it is a holy thing, and cannot be obnoxious to the Lord, or swept away among unholy things; but still the body is subject to pain and weariness, and to the supreme sentence of death. Not so the spirit. There is within us already a part of the resurrection accomplished, since it is written, "and you hath he quickened who were dead in trespasses and sins" (Eph. 2:1). You once were like the ungodly, under the law of sin and death, but you have been brought out of the bondage of corruption into the liberty of life and grace: the Lord having wrought in you gloriously, "according to the working of his mighty power, which he wrought in Christ, when he raised him from the dead, and set him at his own right hand in the heavenly places" (Eph. 1:19, 20).

Now, just as Jesus Christ led, after His resurrection, a life very different from that before His death, so you and I are called upon to live a high and noble spiritual and heavenly life, seeing that we have been raised from the dead to die no more. Let us joy and rejoice in this. Let us behave as those who are alive from the dead, the happy children of the Resurrection. Do not let us be money-grubbers, or hunters after worldly fame. Let us not set our affections on the foul things of this dead and rotten world, but let our hearts fly upward, like young birds that have broken loose of their shells—upward towards our Lord and the heavenly things upon which He would have us set our minds. Living truth, living work, living faith, these are the things for living men: let us cast off the graveclothes of our former lusts, and wear the garments of light and life. May the Spirit of God help us in further meditating upon these things at home.

Bearings of the Resurrection upon the Gospel

Now, secondly, let us consider THE BEARINGS OF THIS FACT OF THE RESURRECTION UPON THE GOSPEL; for Paul says, "Jesus Christ was raised from the dead *according to my gospel.*" I always like to see what way any kind of statement bears on the gospel. I may not have many more opportunities of preaching, and I make up my mind to this one thing, that I will waste no time upon secondary themes, but when I do preach it shall be the gospel, or something very closely bearing upon it. I will endeavor each time to strike under the fifth rib, and never beat the air. Those who have a taste for the superfluities may take their fill of them, it is for me to keep to the great necessary truths by which men's souls are saved. My work is to preach Christ crucified and the gospel, which gives men salvation through faith. I hear every now and then of men preaching sermons about some bright new nothing or another. Some preachers remind me of the emperor who had a wonderful skill in carving men's heads upon cherry stones. What a multitude of preachers we have who can make wonderfully fine discourses out of a mere passing thought, of no consequence to anyone. But we want the gospel. We have to live and die, and we must have the gospel. Certain of us may be cold in our graves before many weeks are over, and we cannot afford to toy and trifle: we want to see the bearings of all teachings upon our eternal destinies, and upon the gospel which sheds its light over our future.

The resurrection of Christ is vital, because first it tells us that *the gospel is the gospel of a living Savior.* We have not to send poor penitents to the crucifix, the dead image of a dead man. We say not, "These be the gods, O Israel!" We have not to send you to a little baby Christ nursed by a woman. Nothing of the sort. Behold the Lord who lives and was dead and is alive forevermore, and has the keys of hell and of death! Behold in Him a living and accessible Savior who out of the glory still cries with loving accents, "Come unto me, all ye that labor and are heavy laden, and I will give you rest" (Matt. 11:28). "He is able also to save them to the uttermost that come unto God by him, seeing he ever liveth to make intercession for them" (Heb. 7:25). I say we have a living Savior, and is not this a glorious feature of the gospel?

Notice next that *we have a powerful Savior* in connection with the gospel that we preach; for He who had power to raise Himself from the dead, has all power now that He is raised. He who in death vanquishes death, can much more conquer by His life. He who being in the grave did, nevertheless, burst all its bonds, can assuredly deliver all His people. He who, coming under the power of the law, did, nevertheless, fulfill the law, and thus set His people free from bondage, must be mighty to save. You need a Savior strong and mighty, yet you do not want one stronger than He of whom it is written that He rose again from the dead. What a blessed gospel we have to preach—the gospel of a living Christ who has Himself returned from the dead leading captivity captive.

And now notice, that *we have the gospel of complete justification* to preach to you. We do not come and say, "Brethren, Jesus Christ by His death did something by which men may be saved if they have a mind to be, and diligently carry out their good resolves." No, no; we say Jesus Christ took the sin of His people upon Himself and bore the consequences of it in His own body on the tree, so that He died; and having died, and so paid the penalty, He lives again; and now all for whom He died, all His people whose sins He bore, are free from the guilt of sin. You ask me, "Who are they?" and I reply, as many as believe on Him. Whosoever believes in Jesus Christ is as free from the guilt of sin as Christ is. Our Lord Jesus took the sin of His people, and died in the sinner's stead, and now being Himself set free, all His people are set free in their Representative. This doctrine is worth preaching. One may well rise from his bed to talk about perfect justification through faith in Christ Jesus. One might as well keep asleep as rise to say that Jesus accomplished little or nothing by His passion and His rising. Some seem to dream that Jesus made some little opening by which we have a slight chance of reaching pardon and eternal life, if we are diligent for many years. This is not our gospel. Jesus has saved His people. He has performed the work entrusted to Him. He has finished transgression, made an end of sin, and brought in everlasting righteousness, and whosoever believes in Him is not condemned, and never can be.

Once again, the connection of the resurrection and the gospel is this, *it proves the safety of the saints*, for if when Christ rose His people rose also, they rose to a life like that of their Lord, and therefore they can never die. It is written, "Christ being raised from the dead dieth no more; death hath no more dominion over him" (Rom. 6:9), and it is so with the believer: if you have been dead with Christ and are risen with Christ, death has no more dominion over you; you shall never go back to the beggarly elements of sin, you shall never become what you were before your regeneration. You shall never perish, neither shall any pluck you out of Jesus' hand. He has put within you a living and incorruptible seed which liveth and abideth forever. He says himself, "The water that I shall give him shall be in him a well of living water springing up unto everlasting life" (John 4:14). Wherefore hold fast to this, and let the resurrection of your Lord be the pledge of your own final perseverance.

Brethren, I cannot stop to show you how this resurrection touches the gospel at ever point, but Paul is always full of it. More than thirty times Paul talks about the resurrection, and occasionally at great length, giving whole chapters to the glorious theme. The more I think of it the more I delight to preach Jesus and the resurrection. The glad tidings that Christ has risen is as truly the gospel as the doctrine that He came among men and for men presented His blood as a ransom. If angels sang glory to God in the highest when the the Lord was born, I feel impelled to repeat the note now that He is risen from the dead.

Bearing of the Resurrection upon Ourselves

And so I come to my last head, and to the practical conclusion: THE BEARING OF THIS RESURRECTION UPON OURSELVES. Paul expressly bids us "Remember" it. "Why," says one, "we don't forget it." Are you sure you do not? I find myself far too forgetful of divine truths. We ought not to forget, for this first day of the week is consecrated for sabbatic purposes to constrain us to think of the resurrection. On the seventh day men celebrated a finished creation, on the first day we celebrate a finished redemption. Bear it, then, in mind. Now, if you will remember that Jesus Christ of the seed of David rose from the dead, what will follow?

First, you will find that *most of your trials will vanish.* Are you tried by your sins? Jesus Christ rose again from the dead for your justification. Does Satan accuse? Jesus rose to be your advocate and intercessor. Do infirmities hinder? The living Christ will show Himself strong on your behalf. You have a living Christ, and in Him you have all things. Do you dread death?

Jesus, in rising again, has vanquished the last enemy. He will come and meet you when it is your turn to pass through the chill stream, and you shall ford it in sweet company. What is your trouble? I care not what it is, for if you will only think of Jesus as living, full of power, full of love, and full of sympathy, having experienced all your trials, even unto death, you will have such a confidence in His tender care and in His boundless ability that you will follow in His footsteps without a question. Remember Jesus, and that He rose again from the dead, and your confidence will rise as on eagles' wings.

Next, remember Jesus, for then you will see how your present sufferings are as nothing compared with His sufferings, and you will learn to *expect victory over your sufferings even as He obtained victory.* Kindly look at 2 Timothy 2, and you will find the apostle there saying in the third verse, "Thou therefore endure hardness, as a good soldier of Jesus Christ," and further on in the eleventh verse, "It is a faithful saying: for if we be dead in him, we shall also live in him: if we suffer, we shall also reign with him." Now, then, when you are called to suffer, think—"Jesus suffered, yet Jesus rose again from the dead; He came up out of his baptism of griefs the better and more glorious for it, and so shall I!" Wherefore go you into the furnace at the Lord's bidding, and do not fear that the smell of fire shall pass upon you. Go you even down into the grave, and do not think that the worm shall make an end of you any more than it did of Him. Behold in the risen One the type and model of what you are and are to be! Wherefore fear not, for Christ conquered! Stand not trembling, but march boldly on, for Jesus Christ of the seed of David rose from the dead, and you who are of the seed of the promise shall rise again from all your trials and afflictions, and live a glorious life.

We see here, dear brethren, in being told to remember Jesus that *there is hope even in our hopelessness.* When are things most hopeless in a man? Why, when he is dead! Do you know what it is to come down to that, so far as your inward weakness is concerned? I do. At times it seems to be that all my joy is buried like a dead thing, and all my present usefulness and all my hope of being useful in the future are coffined and laid underground like a corpse. In the anguish of my spirit, and the desolation of my heart, I could count it better to die than to live. You say it should not be so. I grant you it should not be so, but so it is. Many things happen within the minds of poor mortals which should not happen; if we had more courage and more faith they would not happen. Ay, but when we go down, down, down, is it not a blessed thing that Jesus Christ of the seed of David died, and was raised from the dead? If I sink right down among the dead men yet will I hold to this blessed hope, that as Jesus rose again from the dead, so also shall my joy, my usefulness, my hope, my spirit rise. "Thou, which hast showed us great and sore troubles, shalt quicken us again, and bring us up from the lowest depths of the earth" (Ps. 71:20). This downcasting and slaying is good for us. We take a deal of killing, and it is by being killed that we live. Many a man will never live till his proud self is slain. O proud Pharisee, if you are to live among those whom God accepts, you will have to come to the slaughterhouse and be cut in pieces as well as killed. "This is dreadful work," says one, "this dividing of joints and marrow, this spiritual dismemberment and destruction." Assuredly it is painful, and yet it were a grievous loss to be denied it. Alas, how many are so good and excellent, and strong and wise, and clever, and all that, that they cannot agree to be saved by grace through faith. If they could be reduced to less than nothing it would be the finest thing that ever happened to them.

Remember what Solomon said might be done with the fool, and yet it would not answer—he was to be brayed in a mortar among wheat with a pestle—pretty hard dealing that, and yet his folly would not depart from him. Not by that process alone, but through some such method, the Holy Spirit brings men away from their folly. Under his killing operations this may be their comfort that, if Jesus Christ rose literally from the dead (not from sickness, but from death), and lives again, even so will His people. Did you ever get, where John Bunyan pictures Christian as getting, right under the old dragon's foot? He is very heavy, and presses the very breath out of a fellow when he makes him his footstool. Poor Christian lay there with the dragon's foot on his breast; but he was just able to stretch out his hand and lay hold on his sword, which, by a good providence, lay within his reach. Then he gave Apollyon a deadly thrust, which made him spread his dragon wings and fly away. The poor crushed and broken pilgrim, as he gave the stab to his foe, cried, "Rejoice not over me, O mine enemy; though I fall, yet shall I rise again." Brother, do you the same. You who are near despair, let this be the strength that nerves your arm and steels your heart. "Jesus Christ of the seed of David was raised from the dead according to Paul's gospel" (2 Tim. 2:8).

Lastly, this proves *the futility of all opposition to Christ*. The learned are going to destroy the Christian religion. Already, according to their boastings, it has pretty nearly come to an end. The pulpit is effete, it cannot command public attention. We stand up and preach to empty benches! As you see—*or do not see*. Nothing remains for us but to die decently, so they insinuate. And what then? When our Lord was dead, when the clay-cold corpse lay, watched by the Roman soldiery, and with a seal upon the enclosing stone, was not the cause in mortal jeopardy? But how fared it? Did it die out? Every disciple that Jesus had made forsook Him, and fled, was not Christianity then destroyed? Nay, that very day our Lord won a victory which shook the gates of hell, and caused the universe to stand astonished. Matters are not worse with Him at this hour! His affairs are not in a sadder condition today than then. Nay, see Him today and judge. On His head are many crowns, and at His feet the hosts of angels bow! Jesus is the master of legions today, while the Caesars have passed away! Here are His people—needy, obscure, despised, I grant you, still, but assuredly somewhat more numerous than they were when they laid Him in the tomb. His cause is not to be crushed, it is forever rising.

Year after year, century after century, bands of true and honest hearts are marching up to the assault of the citadel of Satan. The prince of this world has a stronghold here on earth, and we are to capture it; but as yet we see small progress, for rank after rank the warriors of the Lord have marched to the breach and disappeared beneath the terrible fire of death. All who have gone before seem to have been utterly cut off and destroyed, and still the enemy holds his ramparts against us. Has nothing been done, think you? Has death taken away those martyrs, and confessors, and preachers, and laborious saints, and has nothing been achieved? Truly if Christ were dead I would admit our defeat, for they who are fallen asleep in Him would have perished: but as Christ lives so the cause lives, and they who have fallen are not dead: they have vanished from our sight for a little, but if the curtain could be withdrawn every one of them would be seen to stand in his lot unharmed, crowned, victorious! "Who are these arrayed in white robes, and whence came they?" (Rev. 7:13). These are they who were defeated! Whence, then, their crowns? These are they who were dishonored! Whence then their white robes? These are they who clung to a cause which is overthrown. Whence then their long life of victors, for there is not a vanquished man among them all?

Let the truth be spoken. Defeat is not the word for the cause of Jesus, the Prince of the house of David. We have always been victorious, brethren; we are victorious now. Follow your Master on your white horses, and be not afraid! I see Him in the front with His blood-stained vesture around Him, fresh from the wine-press where He has trodden down His foes. You have not to present atoning blood, but only to conquer after your Lord. Put on your white raiment and follow Him on your white horses, conquering and to conquer. He is nearer than we think, and the end of all things may be before the next jibe shall have come forth from the mouth of the last new skeptic. Have confidence in the risen One, and live in the power of His resurrection.

2

*The Ascension of Christ**

Unto every one of us is given grace according to the measure of the gift of Christ. Wherefore he saith, when he ascended up on high, he led captivity captive, and gave gifts unto men. (Now that he ascended, what is it, but that he also descended first into the lower parts of the earth? He that descended is the same also that ascended up far above all heavens, that he might fill all things.) And he gave some, apostles; and some, prophets; and some, evangelists; and some, pastors and teachers; for the perfecting of the saints, for the work of the ministry, for the edifying of the body of Christ (Ephesians 4:7-12).

Our blessed Lord and Master has gone from us. From the mount of Olives, the place where in dread conflict His garments were rolled in blood, He has mounted in triumph to His throne. After having shown Himself for forty days among His beloved disciples, giving them abundant evidence that He had really risen from the dead, and enriching them by His divine counsels, He was taken up. Slowly rising before them all, He gave them His blessing as He disappeared. Like good old Jacob, whose departing act was to bestow a benediction on his twelve sons and their descendants, so before the cloud received our Lord out of our sight, He poured a blessing upon the apostles, who were looking upward, and who were the representatives of His church.

He is gone! His voice of wisdom is silent for us, His seat at the table is empty, the congregation on the mountain hears Him no more. It would be very easy to have found reasons why He should not have gone. Had it been a matter of choice to us, we should have entreated Him to tarry with us till the dispensation closed. Unless, peradventure, grace had enabled us to say: "Not as we will, but as thou wilt," we should have constrained Him, say-

* This sermon is taken from *The Metropolitan Tabernacle Pulpit* and was preached on Sunday morning, March 26, 1871.

ing, "Abide with us." What a comfort to disciples to have their own beloved Teacher visibly with them! What a consolation to a persecuted band to see their leader at their head; difficulties would disappear, problems would be solved, perplexities removed, trials made easy, temptations averted! Let Jesus Himself, their own dear Shepherd be near, and the sheep will lie down in security. Had He been here we could have gone to Him in every affliction, like those of whom it is said, "they went and told Jesus."

It seemed expedient for Him to stay, to accomplish the conversion of the world. Would not His presence have had an influence to win by eloquence of gracious word and argument of loving miracle? If He put forth His power the battle would soon be over, and His rule over all hearts would be forever established. "Thine arrows are sharp in the heart of the king's enemies; whereby the people fall under thee." Go not from the conflict, you mighty bowman, but still cast your all-subduing darts abroad. In the days of our Lord's flesh, before He had risen from the dead, He did but speak, and those who came to take Him fell to the ground; might we but have Him near us no persecuting hand could seize us; at His bidding, the fiercest enemy would retire. His voice called the dead out of their graves; could we but have Him still in the church His voice would awaken the spiritually dead. His personal presence would be better to us than ten thousand apostles, at least, so we dream; and we imagine that with Him visibly among us the progress of the church would be like the march of a triumphant army.

Thus might flesh and blood have argued, but all such reasoning is hushed by our Lord's declaration, "It is expedient for you that I go away: for if I go not away, the Comforter will not come unto you." He might have told us that His majestic presence was expected by the saints in heaven to complete their felicity; He might have said that for Himself it was fitting that after so long an exile and the performance of such stupendous labors, He should rise to His reward; He might also have added that it was due to His Father that He should return into the bosom of His love; but, as if He knew that their trembling at His departure was mainly occasioned by fear for their own personal interests, He puts the consoling word into this form: "It is expedient *for you* that I go away." He has gone then, and whether our weak understandings are able to perceive it or not, it is better for us that Jesus should be at the right hand of God than here corporeally in our assemblies below. Fain would a hundred Bethanies entertain Him, a thousand synagogues would rejoice to see Him open the Scriptures; women there are among us who would kiss His feet, and men who would glory to unloose the latchets of His shoes; but He has gotten Him away to the mountains of myrrh and the hills of frankincense. He no more sits at our tables, or walks with us on our highways; He is leading another flock to living fountains of waters, and let not His sheep below imagine that He has injured them by His removal; unerring wisdom has declared that it is expedient for us that He is gone.

Now, instead of standing here gazing up into heaven, like the men of Galilee, deploring that we have lost our Lord, let us sit down in quiet contemplation, and see if we cannot gather profitable reflections from this great thing which has come to pass. Let our meditations ascend the yet glowing trackway of our Lord's ascension—

> Beyond, beyond this lower sky,
> Up where eternal ages roll.

We shall, by the Holy Spirit's aid, first consider, with a view to practical good, *the fact of His ascension*; secondly, *the triumph of that ascension*; thirdly, *the gifts of that ascension*; and then we shall conclude by noticing *the bearings of that ascension upon the unconverted.*

The Fact of His Ascension

First, then, let our earnest thoughts gaze upward, viewing THE FACT OF THE ASCENSION. We lay aside all controversy or attempt at mere doctrinal definition, and desire to meditate upon the ascension with a view to comfort, edification, and soul profit.

It should afford us supreme joy to remember that He who descended into the lower parts of the earth has now "ascended up far above all heavens." The descent was a subject of joy to angels and men, but it involved Him in much humiliation and sorrow, especially when, after having received a body which, according to the psalmist, was "curiously brought in the lowest parts of the earth," He further descended into the bowels of the earth, and slept as a prisoner in the tomb. His descent on earth, though to us the source of abounding joy, was full of pain, shame, and humiliation to Him. In proportion, then, ought to be our joy that the shame is swallowed up in glory, the pain is lost in bliss, the death in immortality. Did shepherds sing at His descent, let all men sing at His rising. Well deserves the warrior to receive glory, for He has dearly won it. Our love of justice and of Him compels us to rejoice in His rejoicing. Whatever makes the Lord Jesus glad makes His people glad. Our sympathy with Him is most intense; we esteem His reproach above all wealth, and we set equal store by His honor.

As we have died with Him, were buried with Him in baptism, have also risen with Him through the faith of the operation of God who raised Him from the dead, so also have we been made to sit together in the heavenly places, and have obtained an inheritance. If angels poured forth their sweetest minstrelsy when the Christ of God returned to His royal seat, much more should we. Those celestial beings had but slight share in the triumphs of that day compared with us; for it was a man who led captivity captive, it was One born of woman who returned victoriously from Boxrah. We may well say with the psalmist in the sixty-eighth Psalm, to which our text refers, "Let the righteous be glad; let them rejoice before God: yea, let them exceedingly rejoice. Sing unto God, sing praises to His name: extol Him that rideth upon the heavens by His name JAH, and rejoice before Him." It was none other than Christ, bone of our bone and flesh of our flesh; it was the second Adam who mounted to His glory. Rejoice, O believers, as those who shout because of victory, divide the spoil with the strong.

Bruised is the serpent's head,
Hell is vanquish'd, death is dead,
And to Christ gone up on high,
Captive is captivity.

All His work and warfare done,
He into His heaven is gone,
And beside His Father's throne,
Now is pleading for His own:

Sing, O heavens! O earth, rejoice!
Angel harp and human voice,
Round Him, in His glory, raise
Your ascended Savior's praise.

Reflect yet again that from the hour when our Lord left it, this world has lost all charms to us. If He were in it, there were no spot in the universe which would hold us with stronger ties; but since He has gone up He draws us upward from it. The flower is gone from the garden, the first ripe fruit is gathered. Earth's crown has lost its brightest jewel; the star is gone from the night; the dew is exhaled from the morning; the sun is eclipsed at noon. We have heard of some who, when they lost a friend or favorite child, never smiled again for nothing could fill the dreary vacuum. To us it could not be that any affliction should bring us such grief for we have learned to be resigned to our Father's will. But the fact that "Jesus, our all, to heaven is gone" has caused something of the same feeling in our souls; this world can never be our rest now, its power to content us is gone. Joseph is no more in Egypt, and it is time for Israel to be gone. No, earth, my treasure is not here with you, neither shall my heart be detained by you. You are, O Christ, the rich treasure of Your people; and since You are gone, Your people's hearts have climbed to heaven with You.

Flowing out of this is the great truth that "*our conversation is in heaven*; from whence also we look for the Savior, the Lord Jesus Christ." Brethren, inasmuch as Christ is gone, our life is hid with Him in God. To the glory-land our Head is gone, and the life of the members is there. Since the Head is occupied with things celestial, let not the members of the body be groveling as slaves to terrestrial things. "If ye then be risen with Christ, seek those things which are above, where Christ sitteth on the right hand of God. Set your affection on things above, not on things on the earth." Our Bridegroom has gone into the ivory palaces. He dwells in the midst of His brethren. Do we not hear Him calling us to commune with Him? Hear you not His voice, "Rise up my love, my fair one, and come away"? Though awhile our bodies linger here, let our spirits even now walk the golden streets and behold the King in His beauty. Begin, O faithful souls, today the occupation of the blessed, praising God even while you linger yet below; and honor Him if not by the same modes of service as the perfect ones above, yet with the same obedient delight. "Our conversation is in heaven." May you and I know what that means to the fullest. May we take up our celestial burgess-rights, exercise our privileges and avocations as heavenly citizens, and live as those who are alive from the dead, who are raised up together and made partakers of His resurrection life. Since the Head of the family is in the glory, let us by faith perceive how near we are to it, and by anticipation live upon its joys and in its power. Thus the ascension of our Lord will remind us of heaven, and teach us the holiness which is our preparation for it.

Our Lord Jesus Christ has gone from us. We return again to the thought. We cannot speak into His ear and hear His voice reply in those dear accents with which He spoke to Thomas and to Philip. He no longer sits at feasts of love with favored friends, such as Mary and Martha and Lazarus. He has departed out of this world unto the Father, and what then? Why He has taught us by this the more distinctly, that *we must henceforth walk by faith and not by sight*, The presence of Jesus Christ on earth would have been, to a great extent, a perpetual embargo upon the life of faith. We should all have desired to see the Redeemer; but since, a man, He could not have been omnipresent, but could only have been in one spot at one time. We should have made it the business of our lives to provide the means for a journey to the place where He might be seen. Or, if He Himself condescended to journey through all lands, we should have fought our way into the throng to feast our eyes upon Him. And we should have envied each other when the turn came for any to speak familiarly with Him.

Thank God we have no cause for clamor or strife or struggle about the mere sight of Jesus after the flesh; for though once He was seen corporeally by His disciples, yet now after the flesh know we even Him no more. Jesus is no more seen of human eyes; and it is well, for faith's sight is saving, instructing, transforming, and mere natural sight is not so. Had He been here we should have regarded much more the things which are visible, but now our hearts are taken up with the things which are not seen, but which are eternal. This day we have no priest for eyes to gaze upon, no material altar, no temple made with hands, no solemn rites to satisfy the senses. We have done with the outward and are rejoicing in the inward. Neither in this mountain nor in that do we worship the Father, but we worship God, who is a Spirit, in spirit and in truth.

We now endure as seeing Him who is invisible; whom, having not seen, we love; in whom, though now we see him not, yet believing, we rejoice with joy unspeakable and full of glory. In the same fashion as we walk toward our Lord, so walk we toward all that He reveals—we walk by faith, not by sight. Israel, in the wilderness, instructed by types and shadows, was ever prone to idolatry. The more there is of the visible in religion, the more is there of difficulty in the attainment of spirituality. Even baptism and the Lord's Supper, were they not ordained by the Lord Himself, might be well given up, since the flesh makes a snare of them, and superstition engrafts on them baptismal regeneration and sacramental efficacy. Our Lord's presence might thus have become a difficulty to faith, though a pleasure to sense. His going away leaves a clear field for faith; it throws us necessarily upon a spiritual life, since He who is the head, the soul, the center of our faith, hope, and love is no more within the range of our bodily organs. It is poor believing which needs to put its finger into the nail-prints; but blessed is he that has not seen and yet has believed. In an unseen Savior, we fix our trust; from an unseen Savior, we derive on joy. Our faith is now the substance of things hoped for, the evidence of things not seen.

Let us learn this lesson well, and let it never be said to us, "Are you so foolish? Having begun in the Spirit, are you now made perfect by the flesh?" Let us never attempt to live by feeling and evidence. Let us banish from our souls all dreams of finding perfection in the flesh, and equally let us discard all cravings for signs and wonders. Let us not be like the children of Israel, who only believed while they saw the works of the Lord. If our Beloved has hidden Himself from our sight, let Him even hide everything else, if so it pleases Him. If He only reveals Himself to our faith, the eye which is good enough to see Him with is good enough to see everything else with, and we will be content to see by covenant blessings, and all else with that one eye of faith, and no other, till the time shall come when He shall change our faith to sight.

Beloved, let us further reflect *how secure is our eternal inheritance* now that Jesus has entered into the heavenly places. Our heaven is secured to us, for it is in the actual possession of our legal Representative, who can never be dispossessed of it. Possession is nine points of the law, but it absolutely secures completely our tenure under the gospel. He who possesses a covenant blessing shall never lose it, for the covenant cannot be changed, nor its gifts withdrawn. We are heirs of the heavenly Canaan by actual hold and sure title, for our legal Representative, appointed by the highest court of judicature, has entered into possession and actual occupancy of the many mansions of the great Father's house. He has not merely taken possession, but He is making all ready for our reception and eternal inhabitation.

A man who enters a house and claims it, if he has any question about his rights, will not think of preparing it for the inhabitants. He will leave any expenditure of that kind till all doubts are cleared up. But our good Lord has taken such possession of the city of the new Jerusalem for us that He is daily preparing it for us that where He is we may be also. If I could send to heaven some mere human being like myself to hold my place for me till my arrival, I should fear that my friend might lose it. But since my Lord, the King of heaven and the Master of angels, has gone thither to represent all His saints and claim their places for them, I know that my portion is secure. Rest content, beloved, and sing for joy as the apostle's heart did when he wrote, "In whom also we have obtained an inheritance."

Further, if Jesus has gone into the glory, *how successful must our prayers be.* You send a petition to court, and you hope for its success, for it is drawn up in proper style and has been countersigned by an influential person. But, when the person who has backed your plea for you is himself at court, to take the petition and present it there, you feel safer still. Today our prayers do not only receive our Savior's imprimatur, but they are presented by His own hand, as His own requests. "Seeing then that we have a great high priest, that is passed into the heavens, Jesus the Son of God," "let us come boldly unto the throne of grace, that we may obtain mercy, and find grace to help in time of need." No prayer which Jesus urges can ever be dismissed unheard, that case is safe for which He is advocate.

Look up, my soul, with cheerful eye,
See where the great Redeemer stands;
The glorious Advocate on high,
With precious incense in His hands.

He sweetens every humble groan,
He recommends each broken prayer;
Recline thy hope on Him alone,
Whose power and love forbid despair.

Once more, though I feel this theme might detain us long, we must leave it, and remark further that, as we consider Christ ascended, our hearts burn within us at the thought that *He is the type of all His people.* As He was, so are we also in this world; and as He is, so shall we also be. To us, also, there remain both a resurrection and an ascension. Unless the Lord come very speedily, we shall die as He did, and the sepulcher shall receive our bodies for awhile. There is for us a tomb in a garden, or a rest in the Machpelah of our fathers. For us there are winding-sheets and graveclothes; yet like our Lord we shall burst the bonds of death, for we cannot be holden of them.

There is a resurrection morning for us because there was a rising again for Him. Death could as soon have held the Head as the members; the prison doors once taken away, post and bar and all, the captives are set free. Then when we have risen from the dead at the blast of the archangel's trumpet, we shall ascend also, for is it not written that we shall be caught up together with the Lord in the air, and so shall be forever with the Lord? Have courage, brother; that glittering road up to the highest heavens, which Christ has trodden, you too must tread; the triumph which He enjoyed shall be yours in your measure. You, too, shall lead your captivity captive, and amidst the acclamations of angels you shall receive the "well done" of the ever-blessed Father, and shall sit with Jesus on His throne, even as He has overcome and sits with the Father upon His throne.

I have rather given you suggestions for meditation than the meditations themselves. May the Holy Spirit bless them to you; and as you in imagination sit down on Olivet and gaze into the pure azure, may the heavens open to you, and, like Stephen, may you see the Son of Man at the right hand of God.

The Triumph of the Ascension

Let us advance to the second point, and dwell upon it very briefly—THE TRIUMPH OF THE ASCENSION. Psalmists and apostles have delighted to speak upon our Lord's triumphal ascension to the hill of the Lord. I shall not attempt to do more than refer to what they have said. Call to your minds how the psalmist in vision saw the Savior's ascension, and, in the twenty-fourth Psalm, represented the angels as saying: "Lift up your heads, O ye gates; and be ye lift up, ye everlasting doors; and the King of glory shall come in. Who is this King of glory? The Lord strong and mighty, the Lord mighty in battle." The scene is described in rich poetic imagery of the most sublime kind. It evidently teaches us that when our Savior left the sight of mortals, He was joined by bands of spirits who welcomed Him with acclamations and attended Him in solemn state as He entered the metropolis of the universe. The illustration which has usually been given is, I think, so good that we cannot better it.

When generals and kings returned from war in the old Roman ages, they were accustomed to celebrate a triumph. They rode in state through the streets of the capital; trophies of their wars were carried with them, The inhabitants crowded to the windows, filled the streets, thronged the housetops, and showered down acclamations and garlands of flowers upon the conquering hero as he rode along. Without being grossly literal, we may conceive some such a scene as that attending our Lord's return to the celestial seats. The sixty-eighth Psalm is to the same effect: "The chariots of

God are twenty thousand, even thousands of angels: the Lord is among them, as in Sinai, in the holy place. Thou hast ascended on high, thou hast led captivity captive: thou hast received gifts for men; yea, for the rebellious also, that the Lord God might dwell among them." So also in Psalm forty-seven: "God is gone up with a shout, the Lord with the sound of a trumpet." Angels and glorified spirits, saluted our returning Champion; and, leading captivity captive, He assumed the mediatorial throne amidst universal acclamations. "Having spoiled principalities and powers, He made a show of them openly, triumphing over them in it."

Our Lord's ascension was a triumph over *the world.* He had passed through it unscathed by its temptations; He had been solicited on all hands to sin, but His garments were without spot or blemish. There was no temptation which had not been tried upon Him. The quivers of the earth had been emptied against Him, but the arrows had glanced harmlessly from His armor of proof. They had persecuted Him relentlessly. He had been made to suffer all that cruel scorn could invent; but He came forth from the furnace with not the smell of fire upon Him. He had endured death itself with love unquenched and courage invincible. He had conquered by enduring all.

As He rose He was infinitely beyond their reach; though they hated Him no less than before, He had been forty days among them, and yet no hand was outstretched to arrest Him. He had shown Himself openly in divers places, and yet not a dog dare move his tongue. In the clear air, from far above the hills of Salem, He who was once tempted in the desert looked down upon the kingdoms of the earth, which had been shown Him by Satan as the price of sin, and reserved them all as His own by right of merit. He rises above all, for He is superior to all. As the world could not injure His character by its temptations, so no longer could it touch His person by its malice. He has defeated altogether this present evil world.

There, too, He led captive *sin.* Evil had assailed Him furiously, but it could not defile Him. Sin had been laid upon Him, the weight of human guilt was borne upon His shoulders, it crushed Him down, but He rose from the dead, He ascended into heaven, and proved that He had shaken off the load, and left it buried in His sepulcher. He has abolished the sins of His people; His atonement has been so efficacious that no sin is upon Him, the Surety, and certainly none remains upon those for whom He stood as substitute. Though once the Redeemer stood in the place of the condemned, He has so suffered the penalty that he is justified now, and His atoning work is finished forever. Sin, my brethren, was led captive at our Immanuel's chariot-wheels when He ascended.

Death also was led in triumph. Death had bound Him, but He snapped each fetter, and bound death with His own cords.

Vain the stone, the watch, the seal,
Christ has burst the gates of hell;
Death in vain forbids His rise,
Christ hath open'd paradise.

Lives again our glorious King!
"Where, O death, is now thy sting?"
Once He died our souls to save;
"Where's thy victory, boasting grave?"

Our Savior's ascension in that same body which descended into the lower parts of the earth is so complete a victory over death that every dying saint may be sure of immortality, and may leave his body behind without fear that it shall forever abide in the vaults of the grave.

So, too, Satan, was utterly defeated! He had thought that he should overcome the seed of the woman when he had bruised His heel, but lo! as the Conqueror mounts aloft, He breaks the dragon's head beneath His feet. See you not the celestial coursers as they drag the war chariot of the Prince of the house of David up the everlasting hills! He comes who has fought the prince of darkness! Lo! He has bound him in iron fetters. See how He drags him at His chariot wheels, amidst the derision of all those pure spirits who retained their loyalty to the almighty King! Oh, Satan! you were worsted then! You fell like lightning from heaven when Christ ascended to His throne.

Brethren in Christ, *everything that makes up our captivity Christ has led captive.* Moral evil He has defeated, the difficulties and trials of this mortal life He has virtually overcome. There is nothing in heaven, or earth, or hell, that can be thought to be against us which now remains; He has taken all away. The law He has fulfilled; its curse He has removed. The handwriting against us, He has nailed to His cross. All foes of ours He has made a show of openly. What joy there is to us in this triumph! What bliss to be interested in it by the gift of faith in Him!

The Gifts of the Ascension

We may now turn to consider THE GIFTS OF THE ASCENSION. Our Lord ascended on high, and gave gifts to men. What were these gifts which He both received from God and gave to men? Our text says that He ascended that He might fill all things. I do not think this alludes to His omnipresence—in that respect He does fill all things; but allow me to explain, as I receive it, the meaning of the passage, by a very simple figure. Christ descended into the lowest parts of the earth, and thereby He laid the foundations of the great temple of God's praise. He continued in His life laboring, and thereby He built the walls of His temple. He ascended to His throne, and therein He laid the topstone amidst shoutings. What remained then? It remained to furnish it with inhabitants, and the inhabitants with all things necessary for their comfort and perfection. Christ ascended on high that He might do that.

In that sense the gift of the Spirit fills all things, bringing in the chosen, and furnishing all that is necessary for their complete salvation. The blessings which come to us through the ascension, are "for the perfecting of the saints, for the work of the ministry, for the edifying of the body of Christ: till we all come in the unity of the faith, and of the knowledge of the Son of God, unto a perfect man, unto the measure of the stature of the fullness of Christ."

Observe next, that these filling blessings of the ascension are *given to all the saints*. Does not the first verse of our text say: "Unto every one of us is given grace according to the measure of the gift of Christ"? The Holy Spirit is the particular benediction of the ascension, and the Holy Spirit is in measure given to all truly regenerated persons. You have all, my brethren, some measure of the Holy Spirit; some more, some less. But whatever you have of the Holy Spirit comes to you because Christ, when He ascended up on high, received gifts for men that the Lord God might dwell among them. Every Christian having the gift of Christ in His measure, is bound to use it for the general good. For in a body no joint or member exists for itself but for the good of the whole. You, brother, whether you have much grace or little, must, according to the effectual working in you, supply your part to the increase of the body unto the edifying of itself in love. See that you regard your gifts in this light; trace them to Christ, and then use them for the object for which He designed them.

But to some persons the Holy Spirit is given more largely. As the result of the ascension of Christ into heaven the church received apostles, men who were selected as witnesses because they had personally seen the Savior—an office which necessarily dies out, and properly so, because the miraculous power also is withdrawn. They were needed temporarily, and they were given by the ascended Lord as a choice legacy. Prophets, too, were in the early church. They were needed as a link between the glories of the old and new covenant; but each prophetic gift came from the Spirit through the Redeemer's ascent to glory. There remain rich gifts among us still, which I fear we do not sufficiently prize. Among men God's richest gifts are men of high vocation, separated for the ministry of the gospel. From our ascended Lord come all true *evangelists*. These are they who preach the gospel in divers places, and find it the power of God unto salvation. They are founders of churches, breakers of new soil, men of a missionary spirit, who build not on other men's foundations, but dig out for themselves. We need many such deliverers of the good news where as yet the message has not been heard.

I scarcely know of any greater blessing to the church than the sending forth of earnest, indefatigable, anointed men of God, taught of the Lord to be winners of souls. Who among us can estimate the value of George Whitfield to the age in which he lived? Who shall ever calculate the price of a John Williams or a William Knibb? Whitfield was, under God, the salvation of our country, which was going down straight to Pandemonium; Williams reclaimed the islands of the sea from cannibalism; and Knibb broke the Negro's chains. Such evangelists as these are gifts beyond all price.

Then come the *pastors and teachers*, doing one work in different forms. These are sent to feed the flock; they abide in one place, and instruct converts which have been gathered—these also are invaluable gifts of the ascension of Jesus Christ. It is not given unto all men to be pastors, nor is it needed; for if all were shepherds, where were the flock? Those to whom this grace is especially given are fitted to lead and instruct the people of God, and this leading is much required. What would the church be without her pastors? Let those who have tried to do without them be a warning to you.

Wherever you have pastors or evangelists, they exist for the good of the church of God. They ought to labor for that end, and never for their own personal advantage. Their power is their Lord's gift, and it must be used in His way.

The point I want to come at is this. Dear friends, since we all, as believers, have some measure of the Spirit, let us use it. Stir up the gift that is in you. Don't be like the man in the parable who had but one talent and hid it in a napkin. Brother, sister, if you are the least known joint in the body, rob not the body by indolence or selfishness, but use your gift that the body of Christ may come to its perfection. Yet since you have no great personal gifts, serve the church by praying the Lord who has ascended to give us more evangelists, pastors, and teachers. He alone can give them; any who come without Him are impostors. There are some prayers you must not pray, there are others you may pray, but there are a few you *must* pray. There is a petition which Christ has commanded us to offer, and yet I very seldom hear it. It is this one. "Pray ye therefore the Lord of the harvest, that he will send forth laborers into his harvest." We greatly lack evangelists and pastors. I do not mean that we lack muffs, who occupy the pulpits and empty the pews. I believe the market has for many years been sufficiently supplied therewith; but we lack those who can stir the heart, arouse conscience, and build up the church. The scatterers of flocks may be found everywhere; the gatherers of them, how many have we of such? Such a one at this day is more precious than the gold of Ophir. The Queen can make a bishop of the Established Church, but only the ascended Lord can send a bishop to the true church. Prelates, popes, cardinals, vicars, prebends, canons, deans, the Lord has nothing to do with. I see not even the name of them in His Word, but the very poorest pastor whom the Lord ordains is a gift of His ascending glory.

At this moment we are deploring that in the mission field our good men are gray. Duff, Moffat, and the like, are passing from the stage of action. Where are their successors? I was almost about to say, Echo answers, Where? We want evangelists for India, for China, for all the nations of the earth; and though we have many godly fathers among us, who are instructors in the faith, yet have we in all our pastorates few of eminence who could be mentioned in the same day as the great Puritanic divines. If the ministry should become weak and feeble among us, the church richly deserves it, for this, the most important part of her whole organization, has been more neglected than anything else.

I thank God this church has not only prayed for ministers, but has proved the sincerity of her prayer by helping such as God has called, by affording them leisure and assistance for understanding the way of God more perfectly. We have thought that Christ's gifts were valuable enough for us to treasure up and improve them. Our college has now received and sent forth, in the name of Jesus, more than two hundred ministers of the Word. Look around you and see how few churches care to receive the ascension gifts of Christ, and how few pastors encourage young men to preach.

I read the other day, with unutterable horror, the complaint that our churches were like to have too many ministers; an almost blasphemous complaint, impugning the value of Christ's ascension gifts. O that God would give us ten times the number of men after His own heart, and surely there would be then great lack of more! But there are too many, say they, for the present pulpits. Oh, miserable soul! is it come to this, that a minister of Christ must have a pulpit ready to hand? Are we all to be builders on other men's foundations? Have we none among us who can gather their own flocks? In a three-million city like this can any man say that laborers for Christ are too many?

Loiterers are too many, doubtless; and when the church drives out the drones, who shall pity them? While there remain hundreds of towns and villages without a Baptist church, and whole districts of other lands without the gospel, it is idle to dream that of evangelists and teachers we can have too many. No man is so happy in his work as he who presides over a flock of his own gathering, and no pastor is more beloved than he who raised from ruin a destitute church and made it to become a joy and praise in the earth. Pray the Lord to send true pastors and true evangelists. Christ procured them by His ascension. Let us not forget this.

What! shall it be thought that the blessings of the crucifixion are worth the having, and the blessings of the resurrection worth receiving, but the blessings of the ascension are to be regarded with indifference or even with suspicion? No; let us prize the gifts which God gives by His Son, and when He sends us evangelists and pastors, let us treat them with loving respect. Honor Christ in every true minister; see not so much the man as his Master in him. Trace all gospel success to the ascended Savior. Look to Christ for more successful workers. As they come receive them from His hands; when they come treat them kindly as His gifts, and daily pray that the Lord will send to Zion mighty champions of the faith.

The Bearing of Our Lord's Ascension upon Sinners

We shall conclude by noticing THE BEARING OF OUR LORD'S ASCENSION UPON SINNERS.

We will utter few words, but full of comfort. Did you notice in the sixty-eighth Psalm the words: "He received gifts for men; *yea, for the rebellious also*"? When the Lord went back to His throne He had thoughts of love toward rebels still. The spiritual gifts of the church are for the good of the rebels as well as for the building up of those who are reconciled. Sinner, every true minister exists for your good, and all the workers of the church have an eye to you.

There are one or two promises connected with our Lord's ascension which show His kindness to you: "I, if I be lifted up from the earth, will draw all men unto me." An ascended Savior draws you—run after Him. Here is another word of His: "He is exalted on high." To curse? No; "to give repentance and remission of sins." Look up to the glory into which He has entered; ask for repentance and remission. Do you doubt His power to save you?

Here is another text: "He is able also to save them to the uttermost that come unto God by him, seeing he ever liveth to make intercession for them." Surely He has gone to heaven for you as well as for the saints. You ought to take good heart, and put your trust in Him at this happy hour.

How dangerous it will be to despise Him! They who despised Him in His shame perished. Jerusalem became a field of blood because it rejected the despised Nazarene. What will it be to reject the King now that He has taken to Himself His great power? Remember, this same Jesus who is gone up to heaven will so come in like manner as He was seen to go up into heaven. His return is certain, and your summons to His bar equally certain; but what account can you give if you reject Him? O come and trust Him this day. Be reconciled to Him lest He be angry, and you perish from the way while His wrath is kindled but a little. The Lord bless you, and grant you a share in His ascension. Amen, and Amen.

3

The Ascension and the Second Advent Practically Considered[*]

And while they looked stedfastly toward heaven as he went up, behold, two men stood by them in white apparel; which also said, Ye men of Galilee, why stand ye gazing up into heaven? this same Jesus, which is taken up from you into heaven, shall so come in like manner as ye have seen him go into heaven (Acts 1:10,11).

Four great events shine out brightly in our Savior's story. All Christian minds delight to dwell upon His birth, His death, His resurrection, and His ascension. These make four rounds in that ladder of light, the foot of which is upon the earth, but its top reaches to heaven. We could not afford to dispense with any one of those four events, nor would it be profitable for us to forget, or to underestimate the value of any one of them. That the Son of God was born of a woman creates in us the intense delight of a brotherhood springing out of a common humanity. That Jesus once suffered unto the death for our sins, and thereby made a full atonement for us, is the rest and life of our spirits. The manger and the cross together are divine seals of love. That the Lord Jesus rose again from the dead is the warrant of our justification, and also a transcendently delightful assurance of the resurrection of all His people and of their eternal life in Him. Has He not said, "Because I live ye shall live also"? The resurrection of Christ is the morning star of our future glory. Equally delightful is the remembrance of His ascension. No song is sweeter than this—"Thou hast ascended on high; thou hast led captivity captive, thou hast received gifts for men, yea, for the rebellious also, that the Lord God might dwell among them."

---

* This sermon is taken from *The Metropolitan Tabernacle Pulpit* and was preached on Sunday morning, December 28, 1884.

Each one of those four events points to another, and they all lead up to it: the fifth link in the golden chain is our Lord's second and most glorious advent. Nothing is mentioned between His ascent and His descent. True, a rich history comes between; but it lies in a valley between two stupendous mountains: we step from alp to alp as we journey in meditation from the ascension to the second advent. I say that each of the previous four events points to it. Had He not come a first time in humiliation, born under the law, He could not have come a second time in amazing glory "without a sin-offering unto salvation." Because He died once we rejoice that He dies no more, death has no more dominion over Him, and therefore He comes to destroy that last enemy whom He has already conquered.

It is our joy, as we think of our Redeemer as risen, to feel that in consequence of His rising the trump of the archangel shall assuredly sound for the awaking of all His slumbering people, when the Lord Himself shall descend from heaven with a shout. As for His ascension, He could not a second time descend if He had not first ascended; but having perfumed heaven with His presence, and prepared a place for His people, we may fitly expect that He will come again and receive us unto Himself that where He is there we may be also. I want you, therefore, as in contemplation you pass with joyful footsteps over these four grand events, as your faith leaps from His birth to His death, and from His resurrection to His ascension, to be looking forward, and even hastening unto this crowning fact of our Lord's history; for before long He shall so come in like manner as He was seen to go up into heaven.

Today, in our meditation, we will start from the ascension; and if I had sufficient imagination I should like to picture our Lord and the eleven walking up the side of Olivet, communing as they went—a happy company, with a solemn awe upon them, but with an intense joy in having fellowship with each other. Each disciple was glad to think that his dear Lord and Master who had been crucified was now among them, not only alive but surrounded with a mysterious safety and glory which none could disturb. The enemy was as still as a stone: not a dog moved his tongue. His bitterest foes made no sign during the days of our Lord's afterlife below. The company moved onward peacefully toward Bethany—Bethany which they all knew and loved.

The Savior seemed drawn there at the time of His ascension, even as men's minds return to old and well-loved scenes when they are about to depart out of this world. His happiest moments on earth had been spent beneath the roof where lived Mary and Martha and their brother Lazarus. Perhaps it was best for the disciples that He should leave them at that place where He had been most hospitably entertained to show that He departed in peace and not in anger. There they had seen Lazarus raised from the dead by Him who was now to be taken up from them. The memory of the triumphant past would help the tried faith of the present. There they had heard the voice saying, "Loose him, and let him go," and there they might fitly see their Lord loosed from all bonds of earthly gravitation that He might go to His Father and their Father. The memories of the place might help to calm their minds and arouse their spirits to that fullness of joy which ought to attend the glorifying of their Lord.

But they have come to a standstill, having reached the brow of the hill. The Savior stands conspicuously in the center of the group, and, following upon a most instructive discourse, He pronounces a blessing upon them. He lifts His pierced hands, and while He is lifting them and is pronouncing words of love, He begins to rise from the earth. He has risen above them all to their astonishment! In a moment He has passed beyond the olives, which seem with their silvery sheen to be lit up by His milder radiance. While the disciples are looking, the Lord has ascended into mid-air, and speedily He has risen to the regions of the clouds. They stand spell-bound with astonishment, and suddenly a bright cloud, like a chariot of God, bears Him away. That cloud conceals Him from mortal gaze. Though we have known Christ after the flesh, now after the flesh we know Him no more. They are riveted to the spot, very naturally so: they linger long in the place, they stand with streaming eyes, wonder-struck, still looking upward.

It is not the Lord's will that they should long remain inactive; their reverie is interrupted. They might have stood there till wonder saddened into fear. As it was, they remained long enough; for the angel's words may be accurately rendered, "Why have ye stood, gazing up into heaven?"

Their lengthened gaze needed to be interrupted, and, therefore, two shining ones, such as aforetime met the women at the sepulcher, are sent to them. These messengers of God appear in human form that they may not alarm them, and in white raiment as if to remind them that all was bright and joyous; and these white-robed ministers stood with them as if they would willingly join their company. As no one of the eleven would break silence, the men in white raiment commenced the discourse. Addressing them in the usual celestial style, they asked a question which contained its own answer, and then went on to tell their message. As they had once said to the women, "Why seek ye the living among the dead? He is not here, but is risen"; so did they now say, "Ye men of Galilee, why stand ye gazing up into heaven? this same Jesus, which is taken up from you into heaven, shall so come in like manner as ye have seen him go into heaven."

The angels showed their knowledge of them by calling them "men of Galilee," and reminded them that they were yet upon earth by recalling their place of birth. Brought back to their senses, their reverie over, the apostles at once hasten to Jerusalem. The vision of angels has singularly enough brought them back into the world of actual life again, and they obey the command, "Tarry ye at Jerusalem." They seem to say—the taking up of our Master is not a thing to weep about: He has gone to His throne and to His glory, and He said it was expedient for us that He should go away. He will now send us the promise of the Father; we scarcely know what it will be like, but let us, in obedience to His will, make the best of our way to the place where He bade us await the gift of power.

Do you not see them going down the side of Olivet, taking that Sabbath-day's journey into the cruel and wicked city without a thought of fear; having no dread of the bloodthirsty crew who slew their Lord, but happy in the memory of their Lord's exaltation and in the expectation of a wonderful display of His power? They held fellowship of the most delightful kind with one another, and anon entered into the upper room, where in protracted prayer and communion they waited for the promise of the Father. You see I have no imagination. I have barely mentioned the incidents in the simplest language. Yet try and realize the scene, for it will be helpful so to do, since our Lord Jesus is to come in like manner as the disciples saw Him go up into heaven.

My first business will be to consider *the gentle chiding* administered by the shining ones: "Ye men of Galilee, why stand ye gazing up unto heaven?" Secondly, *the cheering description* of our Lord which the white-robed messengers used, "This same Jesus"; and then, thirdly, *the practical truth* which they taught—"This same Jesus, which is taken up from you into heaven, shall so come in like manner as ye have seen him go into heaven."

A Gentle Chiding

First, then, here is A GENTLE CHIDING. It is not sharply uttered by men dressed in black who use harsh speech, and upbraid the servants of God severely for what was rather a mistake than a fault. No; the language is strengthening, yet tender. The fashion of a question allows them rather to reprove themselves than to be reproved; and the tone is that of brotherly love, and affectionate concern.

Notice, that *what these saintly men were doing seems at first sight to be very right.* I think if Jesus were among us now we would fix our eyes upon Him and never withdraw them. He is altogether lovely, and it would seem wicked to yield our eyesight to any inferior object so long as He was to be seen. When He ascended up into heaven it was the duty of His friends to look upon Him. It can never be wrong to look up. We are often bidden to do so. It is even a holy saying of the psalmist, "I will direct my prayer unto thee, and will look up"; and, again, "I will lift up mine eyes unto the hills, from whence cometh my help." If it be right to look up into heaven, it must be still more right to look up while Jesus rises to the place of His glory. Surely it had been wrong if they had looked anywhere—it was due to the Lamb of God that they should behold Him as long as eyes could follow

Him. He is the Sun; where should eyes be turned but to His light? He is the King; and where should courtiers within the palace gate turn their eyes but to their King as He ascends to His throne?

The truth is, there was nothing wrong in their looking up into heaven; but they went a little further than looking—they stood "gazing." A little excess in right may be faulty. It may be wise to look, but foolish to gaze. There is a very thin partition sometimes between that which is commendable and that which is censurable. There is a golden mean as a razor's edge, and He must be wise who does not err either on the right hand or on the left.

"Look" is ever the right word. Why, it is "Look unto me, and be saved." Look, yes, look steadfastly and intently: be your posture that of one "looking unto Jesus," always throughout life. But there is a gazing which is not commendable, when the look becomes not that of reverent worship, but of an overweening curiosity; when there mingles with the desire to know what should be known a prying into that which it is for God's glory to conceal. Brethren, it is of little use to look up into an empty heaven.

If Christ Himself be not visible in heaven, then in vain do we gaze, since there is nothing for a saintly eye to see. When the person of Jesus was gone out of the azure vault above them, and the cloud had effectually concealed Him, why should they continue to gaze when God Himself had drawn the curtain? If infinite wisdom had withdrawn the object upon which they desired to gaze, what would their gazing be but a sort of reflection upon the wisdom which had removed their Lord?

Yet it did seem very right. Thus certain things that you and I may do may appear right, and yet we may need to be chided out of them into something better: they may be right in themselves, but not appropriate for the occasion, not seasonable, nor expedient. They may be right up to a point, and then may touch the boundary of excess. A steadfast gaze into heaven may be to a devout soul a high order of worship, but if this filled up much of our working time it might become the idlest form of folly.

Yet I cannot help adding that *it was very natural.* I do not wonder that the whole eleven stood gazing up, for if I had been there I am sure I should have done the same. How struck they must have been with the ascent of the Master out of their midst! You would be amazed if someone from among our own number now began to ascend into heaven! Would you not? Our Lord did not gradually melt away from sight as a phantom, or dissolve into thin air as a mere apparition. The Savior did not disappear in that way at all, but He rose, and they saw that it was His very self that was so rising. His own body, the materialism in which He had veiled Himself actually, distinctly, and literally rose to heaven before their eyes. I repeat, the Lord did not dissolve, and disappear like a vision of the night, but He evidently rose till the cloud intervened so that they could see Him no more.

I think I should have stood looking to the very place where His cloudy chariot had been. I know it would be idle to continue so to do, but our hearts often urge us on to acts which we could not justify logically. Hearts are not to be argued with. Sometimes you stand by a grave where one is buried whom you dearly loved; you go there often to weep. You cannot help it, the place is precious to you; yet you could not prove that you do any good by your visits. Perhaps you even injure yourself thereby, and deserve to be gently asked the question, "why?" It may be the most natural thing in the world, and yet it may not be a wise thing.

The Lord allows us to do that which is innocently natural, but He will not have us carry it too far; for then it might foster an evil nature. Hence He sends an interrupting messenger: not an angel with a sword, or even a rod; but He sends some man in white raiment—I mean one who is both cheerful and holy, and he, by his conduct or his words, suggests to us the question, "Why stand ye here gazing?" What will be the benefit? What will it avail? Thus our understanding being called into action, and we being men of thought, we answer to ourselves, "This will not do. We must not stand gazing here forever." Therefore we arouse ourselves to get back to the Jerusalem of practical life, where in the power of God we hope to do service for our Master.

Notice, then, that the disciples were doing that which seemed to be right, and what was evidently very natural, but that it is very easy to carry the apparently right and the absolutely natural too far. Let us take heed to ourselves, and often ask our hearts, "Why?"

For, thirdly, notice that *what they did was not after all justifiable upon strict reason*. While Christ was going up it was proper that they should adoringly look at Him. He might almost have said, "If you see Me when I am taken up a double portion of My spirit shall rest upon you." They did well to look where He led the way. But when He was gone, still to remain gazing was an act which they could not exactly explain to themselves and could not justify to others. Put the question thus: "What purpose will be fulfilled by your continuing to gaze into the sky? He is gone, it is absolutely certain that He is gone. He is taken up, and God Himself has manifestly concealed all trace of Him by bidding yonder cloud sail in between Him and you. Why do you still gaze? He told you, 'I go unto my Father.' Why stand and gaze?" Under the influence of great love, we may act unwisely.

I remember well seeing the action of a woman whose only son was emigrating to a distant colony. I stood in the station, and I noticed her many tears and her frequent embraces of her boy; but the train came up and he entered the carriage. After the train had passed beyond the station, she was foolish enough to break away from friends who sought to detain her. She ran along the platform, leaped down upon the railroad and pursued the flying train. It was natural, but it had been better left undone. What was the use of it? We had better abstain from acts which serve no practical purpose; for in this life we have neither time nor strength to waste in fruitless action. The disciples would be wise to cease gazing for nobody would be benefited by it, and they would not themselves be blessed. What is the use of gazing when there is nothing to see? Well, then, did the angels ask, "Why stand ye gazing up into heaven?"

Again, put another question: What precept were they obeying when they stood gazing up into heaven? If you have a command from God to do a certain thing, you need not inquire into the reason of the command. It is disobedient to begin to canvas God's will. But, when there is no precept whatever, why persevere in an act which evidently does not promise to bring any blessing? Who bade them stand gazing up into heaven? If Christ had done so, then in Christ's name let them stand like statues and never turn their heads. But, as He had not bidden them, why did they do what He had not commanded, and leave undone what He had commanded? For He had strictly charged them that they should tarry at Jerusalem till they were "endued with power from on high." So what they did was not justifiable.

Here is the practical point for us: *What they did we are very apt to imitate*. "Oh," you say, "I shall never stand gazing up into heaven." I am not sure of that. Some Christians are very curious, but not obedient. Plain precepts are neglected, but difficult problems they seek to solve. I remember one who always used to be dwelling upon the vials and seals and trumpets. He was great at apocalyptic symbols; but he had seven children and had no family prayer. If he had left the vials and trumpets and minded his boys and girls, it would have been a deal better. I have known men marvelously great upon Daniel, and specially instructed in Ezekiel, but singularly forgetful of the twentieth of Exodus, and not very clear upon Romans the eighth.

I do not speak with any blame of such folks for studying Daniel and Ezekiel, but quite the reverse; yet I wish they had been more zealous for the conversion of the sinners in their neighborhoods, and more careful to assist the poor saints. I admit the value of the study of the feet of the image in Nebuchadnezzar's vision, and the importance of knowing the kingdoms which make up the ten toes, but I do not see the propriety of allowing such studies to overlay the commonplace of practical godliness. If the time spent over obscure theological propositions were given to a mission in the dim alley near the man's house, more benefit would come to man and more glory to God.

I would have you understand all mysteries, brethren, if you could; but do not forget that our chief business here below is to cry, "Behold the Lamb!" By all manner of means read and search till you know all that the Lord has revealed concerning things to come; but first of all see to it that your children are brought to the Savior's feet, and that you are workers together with God in the upbuilding of His church. The dense mass of misery and ignorance and sin which is round about us on every side demands all our powers; and if you do not respond to the call, though I am not a man in white apparel, I shall venture to say to you, "You men of Christendom, why stand you gazing up into the mysteries when so much is to be done for Jesus, and you are leaving it undone?" O you who are curious but not obedient, I fear I speak to you in vain, but I have spoken. May the Holy Spirit also speak.

Others are contemplative but not active—much given to the study of Scripture and to meditation thereon, but not zealous for good works. Contemplation is so scarce in these days that I could wish there were a thousand times as much of it; but in the case to which I refer everything runs into the one channel of thought, all time is spent in reading, in enjoyment, in rapture, in pious leisure. Religion never ought to become the subject of selfishness, and yet I fear some treat it as if its chief end was spiritual gratification.

When a man's religion all lies in his saving his own self, and in enjoying holy things for his own self, there is a disease upon him. When his judgment of a sermon is based upon the one question, "Did it feed *me*?" it is a swinish judgment. There is such a thing as getting a swinish religion in which you are yourself first, yourself second, yourself third, yourself to the utmost end.

Did Jesus ever think or speak in that fashion? Contemplation of Christ Himself may be so carried out as to lead you away from Christ. The recluse meditates on Jesus, but he is as unlike the busy self-denying Jesus as well can be. Meditation unattended with active service in the spreading of the gospel among men well deserves the rebuke of the angel, "Ye men of Galilee, why stand ye gazing up into heaven?"

In certain cases this uneasiness has drawn to itself a wrong expectation of immediate wonders, and an intense desire for sign-seeing. Ah me, what fanaticisms come of this! In America years ago, one came forward who declared that on such a day the Lord would come, and he led a great company to believe his crazy predictions. Many took their horses and fodder for two or three days and went out into the woods, expecting to be all the more likely to see all that was to be seen when once away from the crowded city. All over the States there were people who had made ascension dresses in which to soar into the air in proper costume. They waited, and they waited, and I am sure that no text could have been more appropriate for them than this, "Ye men of America, why stand ye here gazing up into heaven?" Nothing came of it; and yet there are thousands in England and America who only need a fanatical leader, and they would run into the like folly.

The desire to know the times and seasons is a craze with many poor bodies whose insanity runs in that particular groove. Every occurrence is a "sign of the times"—a sign, I may add, which they do not understand. An earthquake is a special favorite with them. "Now," they cry, "the Lord is coming"; as if there had not been earthquakes of the sort we have heard of lately hundreds of times since our Lord went up into heaven. When the prophetic earthquakes occur in divers places, we shall know of it without the warnings of these brethren. What a number of persons have been infatuated by the number of the beast and have been ready to leap for joy because they have found the number 666 in some great one's name. Why, everybody's name will yield that number if you treat it judiciously, and use the numerals of Greece, Rome, Egypt, China, or Timbuctoo.

I feel weary with the silly way in which some people make toys out of Scripture, and play with texts as with a pack of cards. Whenever you meet with a man who sets up to be a prophet, keep out of his way in the future. And when you hear of signs and wonders, turn to your Lord, and in patience possess your souls.

"The just shall live by his faith." There is no other way of living among wild enthusiasts. Believe in God, and ask not for miracles and marvels, or the knowledge of times and seasons. To know when the Lord will restore the kingdom is not in your power. Remember that verse which I read just now in your hearing—"It is not for you to know the times or the seasons." If I were introduced into a room where a large number of parcels were stored up and was told that there was something good for me, I should begin to look for that which had my name upon it, and when I came upon a parcel and I saw in pretty big letters, "*It is not for you*," I should leave it alone. Here, then, is a casket of knowledge marked, "*It is not for you* to know the times or the seasons, which the Father hath put in his own power." Cease to meddle with matters which are concealed, and be satisfied to know the things which are clearly revealed.

The Cheering Description

Secondly, I want you to notice THE CHEERING DESCRIPTION which these bright spirits give concerning our Lord. They describe Him thus—"This same Jesus."

I appreciate the description the more because *it came from those who knew Him.* "He was seen of angels"; they had watched Him all His life long, and they knew Him. When they, having just seen Him rise to His Father and His God, said of Him, "This same Jesus," then I know by an infallible testimony that He was the same, and that He is the same.

Jesus is gone, but He still exists. He has left us, but He is not dead; He has not dissolved into nothing like the mist of the morning. "This same Jesus" is gone up unto His Father's throne, and He is there today as certainly as He once stood at Pilate's bar. As surely as He did hang upon the cross, so surely does He, the self-same man, sit upon the throne of God and reign over creation. I like to think of the positive identity of the Christ in the seventh heaven with the Christ in the lowest deeps of agony. The Christ they spat upon is not the Christ whose name the cherubim and seraphim are hymning day without night. The Christ they scourged is He before whom principalities and powers delight to cast their crowns. Think of it and be glad this day; and do not stand gazing up into heaven after a myth or a dream. Jesus lives; mind that you live also. Do not loiter as if you had nothing at all to do, or as if the kingdom of God had come to an end because Jesus is gone from the earth, as to His bodily presence. It is not all over; He still lives, and He has given you a work to do till He comes. Therefore, go and do it.

"This same Jesus"—I love that word, for "Jesus" means *a Savior*. Oh, you anxious sinners here present, the name of Him who has gone up into His glory is full of invitation to you! Will you not come to "this same Jesus"? This is He who opened the eyes of the blind and brought forth the prisoners out of the prison-house. He is doing the same thing today. O that your eyes may see His light! He who touched the lepers, and raised the dead, is the same Jesus still, able to save to the uttermost. O that you may look and live! You have only to come to Him by faith, as she did who touched the hem of His garment; you have but to cry to Him as the blind man did whose sight He restored. For He is the same Jesus, bearing about with Him the same tender love for guilty men, and the same readiness to receive and cleanse all who come to Him by faith.

"This same Jesus." Why, that must have meant that He who is in heaven is the same Christ who was on earth, but it must also mean that *He who is to come will be the same Jesus that went up into the heaven*. There is no change in our blessed Master's nature, nor will there ever be. There is a great change in His condition:

> The Lord shall come, but not the same
> As once in lowliness He came,
> A humble man before His foes,
> A weary man, and full of woes.

He will be "the same Jesus" in nature though not in condition: He will possess the same tenderness when He comes to judge, the same gentleness of heart when all the glories of heaven and earth shall gird His brow. Our eye shall see Him in that day, and we shall recognize Him not only by the nail-prints, but by the very look of His countenance, by the character that gleams from His marvelous face. And we shall say, "'Tis He! 'tis He! The self-same Christ that went up from the top of Olivet from the midst of His disciples." Go to Him with your troubles, as you would have done when He was here. Look forward to His second coming without dread. Look for Him with that joyous expectancy with which you would welcome Jesus of Bethany, who loved Mary, and Martha, and Lazarus.

On the back of that sweet title came this question, "Why stand ye here gazing into heaven?" They might have said, "We stay here because we do not know where to go. Our Master is gone." But oh, it is the same Jesus, and He is coming again, so go down to Jerusalem and get to work directly. Do not worry yourselves; no grave accident has occurred; it is not a disaster that Christ has gone, but an advance in His work.

Despisers tell us nowadays "Your cause is done for! Christianity is spun out! Your divine Christ is gone; we have not seen a trace of His miracle-working hand, nor of that voice which no man could rival." Here is our answer: We are not standing gazing up into heaven; we are not paralyzed because Jesus is away. He lives, the great Redeemer lives; and though it is our delight to lift up our eyes because we expect His coming, it is equally our delight to turn our heavenly gazing into an earthward watching, and to go down into the city, and there to tell that Jesus is risen, that men are to be saved by faith in Him, and that whosoever believes in Him shall have everlasting life. We are not defeated, far from it. His ascension is not a retreat, but an advance. His tarrying is not for want of power, but because of the abundance of His long-suffering. The victory is not questionable. All things work for it; all the hosts of God are mustering for the final charge. This same Jesus is mounting His white horse to lead forth the armies of heaven, conquering and to conquer.

The Great Practical Truth

Our third point is this, THE GREAT PRACTICAL TRUTH. This truth is not one that is to keep us gazing into heaven, but one that is to make each of us go to his house to render earnest service. What is it?

Why, first, that *Jesus is gone into heaven.* Jesus is gone! Jesus is gone! It sounds like a knell. Jesus is taken up from you into heaven!—that sounds like a marriage peal. He is gone, but He is gone up to the hills whence He can survey the battle; up to the throne, from which He can send us help. The reserve forces of the omnipotent stood waiting till their Captain came, and now that He is come into the center of the universe, He can send legions of angels, or He can raise up hosts of men for the help of His cause. I see every reason for going down into the world and getting to work, for He is gone up into heaven and "all power is given unto him in heaven and in earth." Is that not a good argument—"Go ye *therefore* and teach all nations, baptizing them in the name of the Father, and of the Son, and of the Holy Spirit"?

Jesus will come again. That is another reason for girding our loins, because it is clear that He has not quitted the fight, nor deserted the field of battle. Our great Captain is still heading the conflict; He has ridden into another part of the field, but He will be back again, perhaps in the twinkling of an eye. You do not say that a commander has given up the campaign because it is expedient that he should withdraw from your part of the field. Our Lord is doing the best thing for His kingdom in going away. It was in the highest degree expedient that He should go and that we should each one receive the Spirit. There is a blessed unity between Christ the King and the common soldier in the ranks. He has not taken His heart from us, nor His care from us, nor His interest from us. He is bound up heart and soul with His people and their holy warfare, and this is the evidence of it, "Behold, I come quickly; and my reward is with me, to give every man according as his work shall be."

Then, moreover, we are told in the text—and this is a reason why we should get to our work—that *He is coming in like manner as He departed.* Certain of the commentators do not seem to understand English at all. "He which is taken up from you into heaven shall so come in like manner as you have seen him go into heaven"—this, they say, relates to His spiritual coming at Pentecost. Give anybody a grain of sense, and do they not see that a spiritual coming is not a coming in the same manner in which He went up into heaven? There is an analogy, but certainly not a likeness between the two things.

Our Lord was taken up; they could see Him rise: He will come again, and "every eye shall see Him." He went up not in spirit, but in person: He will come down in person. "This same Jesus shall so come in like manner." He went up as a matter of fact; not in poetic figure and spiritual symbol, but as a matter of fact—"This same Jesus" literally went up. "This same Jesus" will literally come again. He will descend in clouds even as He went up in clouds; and "he shall stand at the latter day upon the earth" even as He stood aforetime.

He went up to heaven unopposed; no high priests, nor scribes, nor Pharisees, nor even one of the rabble opposed His ascension. It were ridiculous to suppose that they could, and when He comes a second time none will stand against Him. His adversaries shall perish; as the fat of rams shall they melt away in His presence. When He comes He shall break rebellious nations with a rod of iron, for His force shall be irresistible that day.

Brethren, do not let anybody spiritualize away all this from you. Jesus is coming as a matter of fact. Get to work and teach the ignorant, win the wayward, instruct the children, and everywhere tell out the sweet name of Jesus. As a matter of fact, give of your substance and don't talk about it. As a matter of fact, consecrate your daily life to the glory of God. As a matter of fact, live wholly for your Redeemer. Jesus is not coming in a sort of mythical, misty, hazy way. He is literally and actually coming and will literally and actually call upon you to give an account of your stewardship. Therefore, now, today, literally not symbolically, personally and not by deputy, go out through that portion of the world which you can reach, and preach the gospel to every creature according as you have opportunity.

For this is what the men in white apparel meant—*be ready to meet your coming Lord.* What is the way to be ready to meet Jesus? If it is the same Jesus who went away from us who is coming, then let us be doing what He was doing before He went away. If it is the same Jesus who is coming, we cannot possibly put ourselves into a posture of which He will better approve than by going about doing good. If you would meet Him with joy, serve Him with earnestness. If the Lord Jesus Christ were to come today, I should like Him to find me at my studying, praying, or preaching. Would you not like Him to find you in your Sunday school, in your class, or out there at the corner of the street preaching, or doing whatever you have the privilege of doing in His name?

Would you meet your Lord in idleness? Do not think of it. I called one day on one of our members, and she was whitening the front steps. She got up all in confusion; she said, "Oh dear, sir, I did not know you were coming today, or I would have been ready." I replied, "Dear friend, you could not be in a better trim than you are: you are doing your duty like a good housewife, and may God bless you." She had no money to spare for a servant, and she was doing her duty by keeping the home tidy: I thought she looked more beautiful with her pail beside her than if she had been dressed according to the latest fashion. I said to her, "When the Lord Jesus Christ comes suddenly, I hope He will find me doing as you were doing, namely, fulfilling the duty of the hour."

I want you all to get to your pails without being ashamed of them. Serve the Lord in some way or other; serve Him always; serve Him intensely; serve Him more and more. Go tomorrow and serve the Lord by helping the poor and the needy, the widow and the fatherless. Serve Him by teaching the children, especially by endeavoring to train your own children. Go and hold a temperance meeting, and show the drunkard that there is hope for Him in Christ. Or go to the midnight meeting and let the fallen woman know that Jesus can restore her. Do what Jesus has given you the power to do, and then you will not stand gazing up into heaven, but you will wait upon the Lord in prayer, and you will receive the Spirit of God, and you will publish to all around the doctrine of "Believe and live." Then when He comes He will say to you, "Well done, good and faithful servant, enter thou into the joy of thy Lord." So may His grace enable us to do. Amen.

4

*Christ the Cure for Troubled Hearts**

And he said unto them, Why are ye troubled? and why do thoughts arise in your hearts? (Luke 24:38).

It seems, from these questions of our Lord, that true believers may come into a troubled state of mind. The eleven were truly Christ's disciples, and even His apostles; yet, when their faith failed them, and they refused to believe the testimony that Christ was risen from the dead, they were troubled in their minds, and tossed to and fro, as on a stormy sea. Unbelief is a great troubler. Our peace comes to us by faith; and if our faith grows weak, our peace of mind is apt to decline, and we are likely to become much disturbed in spirit. If those who are believers, who have passed from death unto life, are sometimes troubled, you may be sure that others are. It is no wonder that they are troubled who have never experienced the grace of God in conversion, and have never felt the joy which Jesus brings to those whom He saves. If every unconverted man could see his true state, he would not dare to give sleep to his eyes, nor slumber to his eyelids, until he had been brought to know the Lord. If you who are living without a Savior realized your lost condition, your pillows would be stuffed with thorns instead of with feathers. I scarcely think that your bread would be sweet to your taste, or that light would be pleasant to your eyes, if you really knew your present condition, and the jeopardy in which your souls are found. I tremble for you; and I shall be glad if you learn to tremble for yourselves and to flee from the wrath to come.

I want, at this time, to speak more particularly to some who are, in a measure, awakened and aroused to their real position before God, and who have been so for a long while. They are not happy; they never will be

* This sermon was taken from *The Metropolitan Tabernacle Pulpit* and was preached on Sunday evening, April 10, 1887.

happy until a very great change comes over them. Yet I do not see why they should not at once have done with doubts, and fears, and troubled thoughts, and enter immediately into rest and peace. I say that I do not see why they should not receive this great blessing; but I see a great many reasons why they should. I can truly say that, when I preach to you, I labor with all my heart and soul to bring you to the cross of Christ. And I have sometimes thought when I have been going home, "That was a poor sermon if it be judged merely by the rules of rhetoric; yet it was such a sermon that, if I could have heard it myself when I was in despair, when I was longing for salvation, it would have been worth a Jew's eye to me, for it would have been the very thing I wanted to show me the road to heaven. It would have been a key to unlock my dungeon door, and to set me at liberty." And I am praying that it may be so now. Every word I speak is steeped in prayer that some of my truly anxious hearers, who would be right if they could, may now end their wanderings at the cross, and have done with their uneasiness and restlessness, and find peace in Jesus Christ the Savior. So, with that object in view, I am going to take the question out of its connection; and though Jesus put it to His eleven apostles, I shall venture to address it to you who are very far from being apostles, who are not yet even disciples, but who at least wish that you were numbered even among the least of God's people. To you I say, in the words of the text, "Why are ye troubled? and why do thoughts arise in your hearts?"

A Question to Consider

And, first, THIS QUESTION IS WORTH CONSIDERING: "Why are ye troubled?" Many of you are troubled, some of you are very greatly troubled, though not always to the same extent. You shake off your anxiety sometimes. Unhappy men that you are, that you should be able to shake off a trouble which is driving you to the Savior! You get out into company, you become immersed in business, and you forget this great sorrow, this sad perplexity; but, after a while, it comes back to you. A little sickness, or a death in the family, or even the east wind and the fogs, with the dullness that often accompanies them, will bring back to you those sorrowful thoughts, and you are again troubled. And you have many questions in your heart; you cannot get rid of them. It has been so with you for months. I know some with whom it has been so for years. They have been attending my ministry, perhaps, or the ministry of some other preacher of the Word, and, after a sermon which has been pressing and personal, they feel dreadfully uneasy. They cannot tell what to make of themselves; and sometimes they have said, "This state of things must come to an end. We cannot any longer endure to have this indefinable something, this mysterious fear which haunts us, and takes away the very joy of life."

It will be a good thing to ask this question, "Why are we so troubled?"

because it would be a great pity to be troubled for nothing. If there is no cause for the anxiety, let us get rid of it. Count it one of the wisest actions to battle with despondency. I do not suppose there is any man in this place who is naturally more inclined to despondency than I am; but when I feel this pressure upon my spirit, I seek to overcome it by hoping in God. I say to myself, "Why art thou cast down, O my soul? and why art thou disquieted within me? hope in God: for I shall yet praise him, who is the health of my countenance, and my God." When I press the question home and find that there is nothing really to disquiet me, I am not disquieted any longer. And I suppose that you are of much the same make as I am, and that, if you look your trouble fairly in the face and you find that there is nothing in it, then you will shake yourself loose from it and come to a cheery state of heart once more.

But suppose that there should be something that ought to cause you anxiety; is it not best at once to make a full investigation of the matter? *It may be that the cure of the evil lies in the search of it.* Here is a man who is half afraid that he has contracted a disease; but, if so, at present it is only in its early stages. Now, if he is a foolish man, he will say, "I shall not trouble about it; if it gets to be much worse, then I will see to it." But if he be a wise, intelligent man, he says, "I must know the ins and outs of this affair. I will go to the best physician I can find, and he shall thoroughly examine me. I will know what these symptoms mean; for, even if there is disease, perhaps it may be nipped in the bud, and my life may yet be saved. If I go to the doctor at once, he may be able to battle with this mischief before it takes a greater hold upon me." I think that he is a very sensible man to say to himself, "Suppose that my health is all wrong. Possibly there is a cure for my malady. I will go and see if I can have this cure."

Remember that the first thing you ought to see to is your soul. Sirs, by all means attend to your health; look well to the title-deeds of your property, make your wills, and so forth. But, first of all, see to the well-being of your immortal nature, for what will you do if you should pass into another world and find yourselves forever shut out from hope? What an awful thing that would be! Therefore, first and foremost, look to that which is to last forever and make your calling and election sure. God help you by His grace to see to this matter this very hour! If there be a cure to be had anywhere, there will be no particular reason for fearing and being troubled if we resolve to go and obtain it. If it is indeed put within our reach, let us stretch out our hand and take it at once, and so end our troubles and questions in the best manner possible by getting the cure for our smart, the heal-all for our soul-sickness.

The disciples, at the time mentioned in our text, were troubled because, when Jesus stood in their midst, they supposed that it was a spirit, a ghost; yet it was no ghost. It was the real living Lord Jesus, whom they afterward handled, who was there. But "they supposed that they had seen a spirit," and therefore "they were terrified and affrighted."

I wonder whether *your present troubles arise out of supposition.* I have known some who have said to me, "I am afraid, sir, and this is my daily trouble that God has never chosen me to eternal salvation. Suppose that, after all, I should not be one of His elect." Is there not as much sense in supposing the one thing as the other? And suppose that you were to leave off supposing; that would be a very sensible thing to do. There is not much good that ever comes by indulging suppositions of that kind; neither you nor I can climb to heaven, and unfold that roll. "The secret things belong unto the Lord our God." Leave that secret thing with Him. I will tell you something in which there is no supposition. Our Lord Jesus Christ says, "Him that cometh to me, I will in no wise cast out." Under no supposable circumstance will Jesus Christ ever cast away a sinner who comes to Him; therefore, kindly leave the supposing alone, and just take the certainty that whoever comes to Christ He will in no wise cast out.

I hear another one say, "But suppose I have committed the unpardonable sin?" To which I answer, "But suppose you have not?" And there is just as much reason for supposing one way as supposing the other. And again I say, suppose you are wise enough to leave off supposing altogether. If you have committed the unpardonable sin, I should really like to know what it is. For, after reading, I think, as much of sound divinity as anybody, I have never yet been able to discover what it is; nor have I ever met with any divine who has even seemed to me to approximate to any sure and certain description of what the unpardonable sin may be. This much I do know about it. It is called a sin that is unto death, and as soon as ever a man commits it, a spiritual death steals over him, so that he never desires mercy, never is conscious of his guilt, and never wishes to find salvation by Jesus Christ. He becomes dead, so dead that it is not merely the sin which is itself unpardonable, but the condition of heart into which it throws the man, so that he never seeks pardon, or even wishes for it. Now, my dear friends, you know that you have not come to that terrible state because you are always restless about your soul's salvation, and always wishing that by some means you might be saved.

Whatever supposition you bring, I believe that I can sweep your supposition away or that it goes to be swept away. Therefore, do not be in doubt or fear because of a supposition. I could bother you with suppositions if I liked to do so. Suppose there were to be an earthquake. Suppose that top gallery were to come tumbling down. Why, I could go on supposing till I had frightened every nervous soul in the place. But what a fool I should be, and what fools you would be to be frightened thereby! I pray you, believe me, that there is enough in the black facts of your case to trouble you without your vexing yourself unnecessarily by suppositions. It used to be thought to be a mark of sanctity for a man to wear a hair shirt and an iron girdle round his waist which covered him with sores. We know better than that now; therefore, why make a hair shirt of suppositions and an iron girdle of pure inventions of your own imagination? Get rid of them all, I beseech you.

But suppose that you have done with suppositions, yet *it may be possible that you are troubled with thoughts.* "Why do thoughts arise in your hearts?" You are unable to get peace because you have certain thoughts in your hearts. Well, what are your thoughts?

"I have been thinking," says one, "perhaps the Bible is not true." Now, when these disciples thought that Jesus Himself was not really there, but that it was only a specter, our Savior said to them, "Handle me, and see." And the best way to prove whether the Bible is true is not to stand and listen to the evil suggestions of skeptics against it, but to hear its own challenge, "Handle me, and see." There is something wonderfully substantial in the religion of Jesus Christ.

To me, it is life, joy, comfort, strength, everything. I do handle it, and I have tried and proved it for myself these many years. But I do not expect my experience to stand in the stead of your own experience of it. Go to Christ with prayer yourself, go to God with repentance yourself, and see whether He does not pardon you, and bless you, and change you, and make a new creature of you; and when He has done that, believe me, you will never again doubt whether the Bible is true. For when it shall have saved you from your fears, rescued you from your sins, and brought you into life and light and liberty, you will be absolutely certain that it is true because you have tried and tested it yourself.

"Oh, but I have a different thought from that!" says another friend. "I think that I cannot be saved because I do not feel all that I ought to feel. I have not had sufficient horror of sin. I have not felt myself to be the worst sinner who ever lived. In fact, I do not think I ever can drag myself down to that state of despair which I have read of as the experience of a great many who have been saved." Now, that is another of your foolish thoughts which you had better give up thinking. Who told you that you must feel a certain degree of anguish? That Book has not told you so, nor has God's preacher; but we are continually telling you that the suffering on account of sin was laid upon the Lord Jesus Christ, that the atonement for human guilt is in His precious blood, and that you may come to Him just as you are. Have we not often tried to draw a line of distinction between repentance, which is the fruit of the Spirit, and despair, which is a temptation of the devil? Many, no doubt, do come to Christ in black despair; but why should you not come with great hopefulness expecting that He will bless you? And if you do so come, depend upon it that He will not send you away empty. Get rid of that foolish thought,

I pray you, and believe in Jesus Christ, my Lord. May the Holy Spirit help you to do so!

Perhaps a third troubled one says, "My thought is, sir, that, if I professed to be a Christian, I should not live up to it." I heard a good reply to that remark from one who came to see me last week. One said to her, "You know, if you make a profession of religion, you must live up to it." "Oh!" she answered, "all the profession I make is that I put my trust in the Lord Jesus Christ, and I put my trust in Him to help me to live up to it. I dare trust Him as far as that." Mind that you do the same, and get rid altogether of the thought that it is you by yourself who have to live up to your profession. Salvation is of the Lord alone; you have to accept grace from Christ for nothing, and He will delight to give it to you. He will delight, also, to continue to give you all the grace you need till He brings you safe home to glory.

Our Lord asked His disciples, "Why are you troubled? and why do thoughts arise in your hearts?" There are some who say, "*It is the feelings that we have in our heart that cause us anxiety*." Well now, what are your feelings? As a rule, I care much more about faith than about feelings. But for once, do tell me what your feelings are, you who are troubled and vexed with anxious thoughts.

"Well, sir," says one, "I am afraid that I shall not be saved." But why not? "Oh, I do not know why; but I am afraid I shall not!" Well, do you not think that you are very foolish? If you will think of it a little, you will be sure that you are; because, when a person says, "I am so fearful," and you ask, "What are you afraid of?" and he says, "Oh, I do not know, but I am so fearful!" you would say to him, "My dear fellow, if you do not know what it is that you fear, then give up being fearful." If you have nothing to be afraid of, do not be afraid, for what can be the reason of it?

"Oh, but, sir," says another, "I feel—well, to make short work of it, I feel that it is too good to be true!" What is too good to be true? "Why, that I may have my sins forgiven simply upon my believing and may now at once become a child of God!" Too good to be true, it is? Well, it would be too good to be true if it came from you. But as it comes from God, nothing is too good to be true of the good and gracious God. He is willing to blot out all your sins if you will but trust to the Lord Jesus Christ. However much you may have transgressed against His laws, He is prepared to pass an act of amnesty and oblivion, and to blot out all your transgressions. Your wanderings, your blasphemies even, He is ready to forgive, more ready to forgive than you are to be forgiven; and He puts it simply thus: "Believe in my son. Trust that he whom I have appointed to save you will save you; and upon your so trusting, your transgressions are forgiven, and you are saved." It is a great message that we have to deliver. Would you have a little gospel from a great God? Would you have a little gospel from the great Savior who was the Son of God, and yet died upon the tree? If it had been less than it is, you would have begun to quibble about its littleness. But now that it is so great, I pray you, do not quarrel with great mercy, but receive it, believe it. Believe it at once, and let your doubts and fears end, from this time forth, through the effectual working of God's gracious Spirit.

I have lingered too long over this first division, yet I hope I have convinced you that the question is worth considering.

A Trouble to Be Examined

The question we have now to consider is this—HAS YOUR TROUBLE ANYTHING TO DO WITH JESUS? This is what our Lord meant by inquiring of His disciples, "Why are you troubled? and why do thoughts arise in your hearts?" Their trouble had to do with Jesus, but they had made a great mistake concerning Him.

"Well," you say, "this subject of Jesus and His salvation, it is all a supernatural business." *Do all supernatural matters frighten you*? "Yes, sir, they do; I am afraid of that which goes beyond the verge of things that can be seen." You will be there yourself before long; whether you are afraid of it or not, you will die. As surely as you are in this Tabernacle, you will have to do with that which is supernatural. You may live a considerable time, perhaps, if you are a young man. But it will seem a very short while when you come to the end of it, and then death, and heaven, and hell, and angels, and God, and the judgment seat, and eternity, will have to be dealt with by you. Oh, it would be a great mercy if you could now get to be familiar with these things! Think where you wish to live forever; you had better learn the language of the country. It would be well for you to begin to understand something of the world to come, for come it will, and there is no putting it off. The strongest man in this place will have to die. It is a reflection which often forces itself upon me that poor, weak, sickly people keep on living, when you thought that they would have been dead years ago; but your fine, strong, healthy men, these are they of whom we hear, "Such an one died at the railway station," or, "Such an one was taken on a sudden, and is gone." Therefore, see to this matter, sir, see to it at once; you will have to deal with the supernatural sooner or later, so had you not better begin now?

"Oh!" say you, "but *this Lord Jesus Christ, in whom you tell me to trust, seems so unreal*. I cannot see Him, and handle Him, as those apostles did. He is so unreal to me." Yes, so the apostles thought, you know, They thought that they saw a ghost; yet there is nothing more real in all the world than our Lord Jesus Christ. I wish that you would seek Him tonight. I wish you would get to that little room of yours, and kneel at your bedside, and cry, "Savior, if You are indeed a Savior, here is a sinner who longs to be saved; come and save me." If you do so, you shall soon find that, though not gripped with the hand or seen with the eye, yet there is no brighter, truer, and more living reality than Jesus Christ, the Son of God.

"But, sir," you cry, "*this believing seems so vague and indistinct.* If you told me something that I had to do, I would try to do it. If I had to go barefoot from here to John-o'-Groat's House, for instance, I should know what that meant, and I would start tomorrow morning, or, if necessary tonight." Yes, I daresay you would; but, after all, there is nothing more vague in your being told to believe in Jesus than there would be in bidding you to walk barefoot to John-o-Groat's House. To believe in Jesus is a most simple matter, easily understood even by a child; it is just to trust Him, that is all. To believe that what is written concerning Him is true, and then to trust yourself entirely to Him, that will save you. See, I have thrown my whole weight upon this platform rail; if that should go down, I shall go down. Do just that with the Lord Jesus, throw your whole weight on Him. If He cannot save you, be lost. I must be lost, I am sure, if He cannot save me. My whole and only hope hangs on that dear hand that was nailed to the cross. My sole trust is in that precious blood which flowed from His pierced side. I risk my eternal destiny with Him and feel that there is no risk whatever in doing so. Now, tell me, is that vague? It seems to me to be very distinct and clear.

"Well," says one, "but, somehow, *Christ seems so unapproachable.* I cannot get at Him." Now, that is the last thing you ought to say, for He will receive you if you breathe only a silent prayer to Him. In the pew down there, sitting on your seat, or standing in the aisle, or away up in the gallery, just speak to Him in your heart, and He will hear you in a moment. Unapproachable? Why, beloved friends, there is nobody so approachable as Christ! A wish will reach Him; a tear has already found Him. He is everywhere present wherever there is any heart that longs to obtain salvation through Him.

Then I fancy that I hear one of you say, "*I feel He is so holy that I, so guilty, cannot come to Him.*" Would you have Him to be unholy, then? If He were so, how could He save you? But, being holy, yet He bids you come to Him; then, why do you not come? Why do you make a barrier out of such a glorious fact as this, that Christ is good, and just, and true? Remember that this also is true, that Jesus Christ came into the world to save sinners. If He does not save sinners, then He came into this world to mock us. He came into this world for nothing. And if you, being a sinner, will come to Christ, and Christ rejects you, He has forgotten His commission, He has belied His character. He must give up His name, for He is no longer Jesus if He does not save sinners who come to Him, ay, and if He does not save sinners who do not come to Him, too, for He has come to seek and to save—both to seek and to save—that which was lost.

"But," says yet another, "*I cannot think that the Lord Jesus Christ would take any notice of me.*" Oh, that I could nail your wretched, miserable thoughts of my great Lord up on His cross! "Oh, but I am nobody, sir!" Christ died for nobodies. "But I am poor." "The poor have the gospel preached to them." "But I am quite illiterate." Yes, and it is to such that a plain gospel is sent by our gracious Savior. "But I am altogether obscure and unknown." Oh, no, you are not; the Lord Jesus knows all about you! Even the hairs of your head are all numbered. Do not suppose that, if you were rich, Christ would think any more of you than He does now. You know how it is among men; if a man wears a good coat and a diamond ring, people give him a seat directly as he comes into the aisle. Ay, but that is not the spirit of Jesus Christ! He does not care about your diamond rings and your satin dresses. My Lord Himself wore a smock frock, woven from the top throughout, a garment without seam. He was dressed as the plainest and humblest of peasants dressed, and He delighted to associate with the poorest of the poor. Therefore, do not tell me that He will not condescend to look at you. My Lord would leave off listening to the songs of angels to hear a poor sinner cry. If it were some grand review day in heaven, when helmed cherubim and mailed seraphim marched before His august eye, He would quit the camp of angels to come and listen to a beggar's prayer. For, remember, He is a man as truly as He is God, and everything human touches that true heart of His that was pierced for men. Therefore, cry to Him. Ask Him to have mercy upon you. He will stand still, as He did when blind Bartimæus cried to Him, and will command you to be brought before Him. Then He will say to you, "What wilt thou that I should do to you?" And He will give you spiritual sight and spiritual health in answer to your prayer. Come to Him, however poor, and weak, and insignificant you may be, and you shall soon prove that it is even as I say.

If you have made any mistakes about my Lord and Master, I hope that what I have said may help to remove them.

A Conclusion to Be Reached

Now, lastly, and may God bless this word to you, dear troubled friend, to bring you to the Savior! JESUS RIGHTLY KNOWN WILL MEET EVERY TROUBLE OF EVERY SEEKING SOUL. If you did but know Him, you would find an end to your trouble at once. Those lines are quite true:

> His worth is all the nations knew,
> Sure the whole world would love Him too.

If men did but know what a Savior He is, they would never rest till they had proved Him to be their Savior.

Let me tell you a few things that may help to end all your troubles. First, *Jesus Christ is alive.* He died, but He rose again. He is alive, and living among men. Spiritually, He is still on earth. His bodily presence is in heaven, but His spiritual presence is everywhere.

> Where'er we seek Him, He is found.

He is alive, active, living, present with us here; giving us His benedictions; working out His divine projects; a living present force among the myriads of this city; a living present Person in this house of prayer.

Next, *Jesus Christ lives as One who has made a full atonement for sin*. Do you know what that means? This is what I understand by atonement. We were guilty, we had sinned; and the law of God has bound punishment to sin with iron clamps. I am sure that the only way in which the world is to be governed is by this law, that the consequences of evil must be evil. If men will do wrong, they must be punished. With all reverence, we may say that God Himself cannot reverse that law, for it is a right and proper law. Well, then, Jesus Christ came and bore the consequences of human sin in His own body on the tree. Those who believe in Jesus Christ, by the very act of believing, accept Him to be their Substitute, bearing their guilt and punishment, and being unto God a sacrifice instead of them. Therefore, as many as have believed in Jesus Christ may know of a surety that He died in their room, and place, and stead.

I recollect talking one day to a poor man, an Irishman, and trying to make this point very plain to him. I said, "Now suppose you had committed a murder, and you were to be hanged for it." "Yes," he replied, "and I should deserve it." "But suppose I should go to the Queen, and say to her, I am willing to be hanged instead of this man. Such is my love for him that, to set him free and yet to honor the law, I will consent to die in his stead." The man said, "That would be very kind of you, sir." "Well, suppose that the Queen had the ability to consent to it, and I could be accepted as your substitute, and I were hanged instead of you. Would the policeman take you up for that murder?" "Oh, no!" he exclaimed. "I should say, 'You can't touch me. Why, the gentleman was hanged instead of me! Therefore, I am clear.'"

That is exactly the way of salvation. Jesus Christ suffered in the stead of all of you who trust in Him, and you are clear before the bar of divine justice. Every man who believes in Jesus Christ, that is, trusts Him, may know without doubt that Christ was for him a certain and effectual Substitute, by which his sin was put away on the cross. "Who his own self bare our sins in his own body on the tree." Now, if you understand that great truth, I think your doubts and fears ought to come to an end at once.

Remember also that *Jesus Christ lives to give repentance and remission of sins*. In this very chapter, we read that He bade His apostles go and preach repentance and remission of sins in His name among all nations. He says to you, "Turn from your sin, and I will turn from My anger. Quit your sin, and your sin is forgiven. Leave it; loathe it; and I will grant you immediate pardon for the sake of the great atoning sacrifice." This truth also, if it be fully believed, should bring peace and joy to your heart and mind.

Please to recollect, too, that *the Lord Jesus Christ lives to pray for sinners.* He lives to make intercession for the transgressors. He lives to give to sinners the Holy Spirit to work in them true belief and true repentance. He lives, mighty to save, to do for you what you cannot do for yourself, to bear you up, and bear you through, and bring you at last to His own right hand.

Brothers and sisters, as I trust my Lord Jesus Christ myself with all my heart, with all my future, my past, my present, with, indeed, everything, and as I feel perfect peace in so doing, I would to God that you would do the same that you might feel the like peace and get strength within to bear the troubles of this mortal life. Did you ever hear what good John Hyatt, who used to preach to the sailors, said when he was dying? Someone asked him, "Mr. Hyatt, can you trust Jesus with your soul now?" "Trust Jesus with my soul!" he exclaimed, "If I had ten thousand souls, I could trust them all with Him."

We are not ten thousand here right now, we are somewhat under that number. But oh, that we might all come and trust our souls with Jesus! Then, in that last great day, with sweet clamor of praise, with united tempests of song, we will bless that dear crucified but now exalted Savior who will not fail one of us, but will bring us to see His face in glory. Will you not trust Him? Dear friend, you might go down those stairs, you know, with a firm foot, saying, "I am a saved man." Yes, out of this area many a troubled heart may make its way and go home with all the bells ringing out sweet hallelujahs: "I have believed. I am forgiven. I am the chief of sinners, but I am forgiven, for I have trusted where God bids me trust. And now, because I am forgiven, and am a child of God, I will live a new life and will serve the Lord with all my heart."

You good soldiers who are here, I hope you are already good soldiers of Jesus Christ. But if you are not, I would like to be the recruiting sergeant and enlist you beneath the standard of the cross. Only trust my Lord, and you shall be saved in the day of battle, and saved in the hour of death, ay, and saved amidst the temptations of this wicked city. He shall cover you. He Himself shall cover you, and you shall be perfectly safe beneath that divine shelter. Who will trust Christ and be saved? Lord, give us many souls tonight, for Jesus Christ's sake! Amen.

5

*The Two Draughts of Fishes**

Now when he had left speaking, he said unto Simon, Launch out into the deep, and let down your nets for a draught (Luke 5:4).

And he said unto them, Cast the net on the right side of the ship, and ye shall find. They cast therefore, and now they were not able to draw it for the multitude of fishes (John 21:6).

Christ's whole life was a sermon. He was a prophet mighty in word and deed; and by His deeds as well as His words He taught the people. It is perfectly true that the miracles of Christ attest His mission. To those who saw them they must have been evident proof that He was sent of God. But we ought not to overlook that probably a higher reason for the miracles is to be found in the instruction which they convey. To the world without, at the present time, the miracles of Christ are more hard to believe than the doctrine which He taught. Skeptics turn them into stones of stumbling, and when they cannot criticize the marvelous teaching of Jesus, they attack the miracles as monstrous and incredible.

I doubt not that even to minds seriously vexed with unbelief, the miracles, instead of being helps to belief, have been trials of faith. Few indeed there are in whom faith is wrought by signs and wonders; nor indeed is this the gospel way of bringing conviction to the soul. The secret force of the living word is the chosen instrumentality of Christ, and wonders are left to be the resort of that Anti-Christ by whom the nations shall be deceived. We, who by grace have believed, view the miracles of Christ as noble attestations to His mission and divinity, but we confess that we value them even more as instructive homilies than as attesting witnesses. It is our conviction that we should lose much of the benefit which they were meant to convey to us if we were merely to view them as seals to the roll, for they are a part of the writing of the roll itself.

* This sermon is taken from *The Metropolitan Tabernacle Pulpit* and was preached on Sunday morning, April 6, 1862.

The marvels wrought by our blessed Lord are acted sermons fraught with holy doctrine, set forth to us more vividly than it could have been in words. We start with the assumption upon which our sermon will be grounded—that Christ's miracles are sermons preached in deeds, visible allegories, truths embodied, principles incarnated and set in motion. They are, in fact, the pictures in the great book of Christ's teaching; the illustrations by which He flashed light into dim eyes.

We have heard of some ministers who could say that they had often preached from the same text, but they had never delivered the same discourse. The like may be said of Christ. He often preached upon the same truth, but it was never precisely in the same manner. We have read in your hearing the narrative of two miracles (Luke 5 and John 21) which seem to the casual observer to be precisely alike. But he who shall read diligently and study carefully will find that though the text is the same in both, yet the discourse is full of variations. In both the miraculous draughts of fishes, the text is the mission of the saints to preach the gospel—the work of man-catching—the ministry by which souls are caught in the net of the gospel and brought out of the element of sin to their eternal salvation.

The preacher is compared to a fisherman. The fisherman's vocation is a toilsome one; woe be to that minister who finds his calling to be otherwise. The fisherman must go forth in rough weathers, and at all hazards; if he should only fish in a calm sea he may often starve. So the Christian minister, whether men will receive the word with pleasure, or reject it with anger and wrath, must be ready to imperil reputation and risk comfort; yea, he must hate his own life also, or he is not worthy of the heavenly calling. The fisherman's is a rough occupation; no dainty fingers may come in contact with his net. One sermon makes not a preacher; he who shall but now and then deliver himself of some carefully prepared oration is no true minister of God. He must be instant in season and out of season; he must cast his net in all waters; he must be at his work in the morning, and in the evening he must not withhold his hand. To be a fisherman, a man must expect disappointments; he must often cast in the net and bring up nothing but weeds. The minister of Christ must reckon upon being disappointed; and he must not be weary in well-doing for all his disappointments, but must in faith continue in prayer and labor, expecting that at the end he shall receive his reward. No great labor is needed for you to work out at leisure the comparison between fishermen and the gospel ministry, the simile is so aptly chosen.

The two narratives before us have a degree of uniformity; that shall be our first point. *But they have a greater degree of dissimilarity*; we will bring that out in the second place. And, then, thirdly, we will suggest *some great lessons which they both combine to teach us.*

Their Areas of Uniformity

First, then, IN THESE TWO MIRACLES THERE ARE MANY POINTS OF UNIFORMITY. They are both intended to set forth the way in which Christ's kingdom shall increase.

1. First you will perceive that in both miracles we are taught that *the means must be used.* In the first case, the fish did not leap into Simon's boat to be taken; nor, in the second case, did they swarm from the sea and lay themselves down upon the blazing coals that they might be prepared for the fisherman's feast. No, the fishermen must go out in their boat, they must cast the net; and after having cast the net, they must either drag it ashore, or fill both boats with its contents. But yet neither the fisherman, nor his boat, nor his fishing tackle are ignored; they are all used and all employed. Let us learn that in the saving of souls God uses means; that so long as the present economy of grace shall stand, God will be pleased by the foolishness of preaching to save them who believe.

Every now and then there creeps up in the church a sort of striving against God's ordained instrumentality. I marked it with sorrow during the Irish Revival. We constantly saw in some excellent papers remarks which I thought exceedingly injurious, wherein it was made a subject of congratulation that no man was concerned in the work, no eminent preacher, no fervent evangelist; the whole was boasted to be conducted without human instrumentality. That was the weakness of the Revival, not its strength. You say it gave God the more glory. Not so. God gets the most glory through the use of instruments. When God works without instruments, doubtless He is glorified; but He knows Himself in which way He gets the most honor, and He has Himself selected the plan of instrumentality as being that by which He is most magnified in the earth. We have this treasure. How? Alone? Without any earthly accompaniment? No; but in earthen vessels. What for? That God may have less glory? No; but in the earthen vessels on purpose "that the excellency of the power may be of God," and not of us. God makes the infirmity of the creature to be the foil to the strength of the Creator. He takes men who are nothing in themselves and works by them His splendid victories. Perhaps, we should not admire Samson so much if he had dashed the Philistines in pieces with his fist, as we do when we find that with such a weapon, so unadapted to the work, as the jaw-bone of an ass, he laid on heaps the thousands of his foes.

The Lord takes weak weapons that with them He may work great deeds. When He said, "Let there be light, and there was light" without any instrument, He showed His glory. But when instead thereof He takes the apostles and says again, "Let there be light," and sends *them* forth who were darkness in themselves, and makes them the medium of lighting up a dark world, I say there is a greater glory. And if the morning stars sang together when they first saw light upon the new-made earth, surely the angels in heaven rejoiced yet more when they saw light thus streaming upon the dark earth through men, who, in and of themselves, would only have increased the blackness and made the gloom more dense. God works by means of men whom He specially calls to His work, and not as a rule without them. The Plymouth-ist strives to get rid of the pastorate, but he never can. For the Lord will ever continue to give pastors after His own heart to feed His people, and all attempts made by the flock to dispense with these pastors will lead to leanness and poverty of soul.

The outcry against the "one man ministry" comes not of God, but of proud self-conceit, of men who are not content to learn they have no power to teach. It is the tendency of human nature to exalt itself which has raised up these disturbers of the peace of God's Israel. For they will not endure to submit themselves to the authorities which God has Himself appointed, and abhor the teachings of the apostle, where He says, by the Spirit of God, "Obey them that have rule over you, and submit yourselves: for they watch for your souls, as they that must give account, that they may do it with joy, and not with grief: for that is unprofitable to you." Brethren, I warn you, there is a spirit abroad which would pull down the men whom God Himself has raised up, that would silence those into whose mouths God has put the tongue of fire, that foolish men might prate according to their own will to the profit of no one and to their own shame. As for us, we shall, I trust, never cease to recognize that agency by which the Lord works mightily among us.

We would check no ministry in the church of God. We would but be too glad to see it more abundantly exercised. Would God that all the Lord's servants were prophets! But we enter our solemn protest against that spirit which, under pretense of liberty to all, sets aside the instrumentality by which the Lord especially works. He will have you still keep the fishermen to their nets and to their boats; and your new ways of catching fish without nets, and saving souls without ministers, will never answer, for they are not of God. They have been tried, and what has been the result of the trial? I do not know a church in existence that has despised instrumentality, but it has come to an end within a few years either by schism or decay. Where upon the face of the earth is there a single church that has existed fifty years where God's chosen instrumentality of ministry has been despised and rejected? "Ichabod!" is written upon their walls. Their attempts are flashes in the pan, meteoric lights, will-o'-the-wisps, swellings of proud flesh, bubbles of foam, here today and gone forever on the morrow.

2. Again, in both our texts there is another truth equally conspicuous, namely, that *means of themselves are utterly unavailing*. In the first case you hear the confession, "Master, we have toiled all the night and have taken nothing." In the last you hear them answer to the question, "Children, have ye no meat?" "No"—a sorrowful No. What was the rea-

son of this? Were they not fishermen plying their special calling? Verily, they were no raw hands; they understood the work. Had they gone about the toil unskillfully? No. Had they lacked industry? No, they had *toiled.* Had they lacked perseverance? No, they had toiled *all the night.* Was there a deficiency of fish in the sea? Certainly not, for as soon as the Master comes there they are by shoals.

What, then, is the reason? Is it not because there is no power in the means of themselves apart from the presence of Christ? The Great Worker who does not discard the means would still have His people know that He uses instrumentality, not to glorify the instrument, but for the sake of glorifying Himself. He takes weakness into His hands and makes it strong, not that weakness may be worshiped, but that the strength may be adored which even makes weakness subservient to His might.

Brethren, let us as a church always keep this in mind, that without Christ we can do nothing. "Not by might, nor by power, but by my Spirit, saith the Lord." Put no dependence upon societies, upon committees, upon ministries, upon anything that we can do. Let us work as if it all depended upon us; but let us come to God depending upon Him, knowing of a surety that it does not rest with us, but with Him alone. Let us send forth the missionaries to the heathen; let us send forth our men into the dark streets and lanes of London; let us scatter tracts; let us distribute the Word of God; let us send forth preachers by scores from our "School of the Prophets"; but when this is done, let us not sit still and say, "Now it is all accomplished, good must come of it." No, Lord, unless Your blessing descend from on high, as well might we have done nothing, for no eternal results can follow.

How often this drives me to my knees. The surprising work which God is doing in connection with this place lifts up my heart with joy; but then the fear lest it all should come to nothing for lack of His blessing casts my spirit to the very earth. You will remember, I dare say, that one brother was moved some time ago to distribute a volume of the sermons preached here to every student in Oxford and Cambridge. After that had been done, and some two hundred thousand sermons had been distributed, he then gave them to every member of Parliament, to every peer of the realm, and to princes, kings, and emperors of Europe. Having accomplished that work, he has another in hand of great magnitude. Dear friends, as I think of these books traveling everywhere among high and low, the rich and poor in all places of the land, my heart is glad. But then, if God withholds the blessing, as well had they never been born in the press and circulated by human hand, what good can they do?

Let the net be never so broad, never so strong, and let it be never so industriously cast into the sea, yet we shall toil all the night and take nothing unless the Master comes to own the work. Let us, then, be always in prayer for the blessing. Let us remember that we have done nothing until we have prayed over what we have done, let us consider that all the seed we have put into the ground is put there for worms to eat, unless we have dropped into the soil the preserving grain of prayer to keep that other grain alive. We shall have harvest if we wait on God for them, but after all our sowing, if we look to the soil, the seed, or the sower, we shall see nothing for our pains.

3. Thirdly, there is clearly taught in both these miracles the fact that it is *Christ's presence that confers success.* Christ sat in Peter's boat. It was His will that by a mysterious influence drew the fish to the net, as though He had a hook, a secret hook in each of their jaws, could stop them in their sportive leapings, and hurry them all to one common center. It was His presence on the dry land, when He spoke from off the shore to His toiling disciples out yonder, and said, "Cast the net on the right side of the ship"—it was His presence that drew the fish to the place where they were taken. Oh, brethren, we must learn this: that it is Christ's presence in the midst of the church that is the church's power—"I, if I be lifted up, will draw all men unto me." There is the attraction. The Spirit gives the power, and we must tarry until we get it; but when we have it, then we cannot preach in vain, for we become "a savor of life unto life" to those who hear.

Christians, Christ's presence with you must be your power. Be much in fellowship with Him; catch much of His Spirit; meditate much upon His sufferings; keep close to His person; and then, wherever you go there shall be a power about you which even your adversaries shall be compelled to acknowledge. O that we had more of Christ's presence in us as a church! Lift up your hearts for it. If Christ be here at all, let us not grieve Him. "I charge you, O ye daughters of Jerusalem, that ye stir not up nor awake my love till he please." And, if He be not here, let us rise from the bed of our sloth and go forth and seek Him, crying, "O thou whom my soul loveth, tell me where thou feedest, where thou makest thy flock to rest at noon!" And if you find Him, I charge you hold Him, and let Him not go till you bring Him into our mother's house, into the chamber of her that bare us, even the Church of Christ; there will we hold Him, there will we embrace Him, and He shall show to us His loves.

4. In both instances *the success* which attended the instrumentality through Christ's presence *developed human weakness.* We do not see human weakness more in non-success than in success. In the first instance, in the success you see the weakness of man, for the net breaks and the ships begin to sink, and Simon Peter falls down with—"Depart from me for I am a sinful man, O Lord." He did not know so much about that till his boat was filled; but the very abundance of God's mercy made him feel his own nothingness. In the last case, they were scarcely able to draw the net because of the multitude of fishes.

Brethren, if you or I would know to the fullest extent what utter nothings we are, if the Lord shall give us success in winning souls we shall soon find it out. As we see first one, and then another, and then scores, and then hundreds brought to the Lord Jesus, we shall say, "How can such wonders be wrought by me?" And we shall fall prostrate before the footstool of sovereign grace, and confess that we are unworthy of such amazing favors. Let the church spread, let her conquests be many, let her overrun whole provinces with her heavenly arms, and instead of man becoming more famous, man shall sink lower and lower, and it shall be more and more fully perceived that it is the Lord. Little works, such as have been common in our churches for years, where twos and threes are added, are quite consistent with great self-congratulation, and so is utter barrenness; mark the pompous carriage of many a fruitless preacher and see if it be not so. Let the Lord make bare His arm and the man humbles himself in the dust, for when hundreds are ingathered, this cannot be the minister, this is the finger of God. The Lord alone is magnified in that day.

O that God would do in the churches of England some great and stupendous works by all His ministers! Then would they discover their own weakness, and then would the name of God be glorified. You frequently meet with the observation, if a man be successful in winning souls, "I am afraid he will grow proud. How we ought to pray that he may be kept humble!" Brethren, that is a very necessary prayer for anybody; but it is no more necessary for the man who is successful than for the unsuccessful one; in fact, it is an assumption of pride on any person's part to think that he has less need to pray against pride than any other man. Think not that when the church prospers it becomes necessarily proud. No, the very fullness of the boat makes it sink, and the very abundance of the miracle makes us cry out the more, "It is the Lord," for we feel that it could not have been of man, for it is out of man's reach to have accomplished such wonders.

So far, then, there is a likeness running through the whole. Means must be used; means alone, unavailing; Christ's presence gives the success; that success develops human weakness, and leads to the exclamation—"It is the Lord."

Their Areas of Dissimilarity

Having, then, shown the likeness, you will be still more interested in THEIR AREAS OF DISSIMILARITY. We think the first picture represents the church of God as we see it; the second represents it as it really is. The first pictures to us the visible, the second the invisible. Luke tells us what the crowd see; John tells us what Christ showed to His disciples alone. The first is common truth which the multitude may receive, the next is special mystery revealed only to spiritual minds. Observe, then, carefully, the points of divergence.

1. First, there is a difference in the orders given. In the first, it is, "Launch out into the deep, and let down your nets for a draught." In the

second it is, "Cast the net on the right side of the ship." The first is Christ's order to every minister; the second is the secret work of His Spirit in the Word. The first shows us that the ministry is to fish anywhere and everywhere. All the orders that the Christian has, as to his preaching, is, "Launch out in to the deep, and let down your net." He is not to single out any particular character; he is to preach to everybody, sensible sinners and insensible sinners; he is to preach to the dead dry bones of the valley as well as to the living souls. He is not to look where the fish are, but just to throw the net in, doing as his Master tells him. "Go ye into all the world, and preach the gospel to every creature."

Those ministers who preach only to the elect should remember this: our business is to include all sorts of fish, and not to be particular about where we are, but just splash the net in. What if we be in town, or city, or village? What if we be among the rich or poor, learned or illiterate? What if we be among the debauched or immoral? We have nothing to do with that—our duty is the same, to "launch out into the deep, and let down the net"—that is all. Christ will find the fish. It is no business of ours. The secret truth is, that when we are doing this, the Lord knows how to guide us so that we "cast the net on the right side of the ship." That is the secret and invisible work of the Spirit, whereby He so adapts our ministry, which is in itself general, that He makes it particular and special.

We speak to all, and He speaks to some. We blow the trumpet, but only the bankrupt debtors hear it. Only those who are truly of the Spirit of God know the joyful sound and rejoice therein. *We* cannot single them out, but God can. We thrust in the blessed loadstone of the gospel and that heavenly magnet has an affinity to some hearts which God has quickened, so that as many as were ordained unto eternal life believe. The apostles preached to the crowd, but the Lord God the Holy Spirit, who had decreed the salvation of His chosen, sent the word home with power to the chosen and separated ones. What a joy it is to think that we always have a picked congregation here for the Lord has picked them! Though they are crowded together promiscuously—here the good and there the bad, all sorts mingled and mixed together—yet God brings them in according to His eternal purpose, and all the while there is a core of chosen souls inside the mass of the congregation to whom God is applying the Word. We cast the net, after all, on the right side of the ship, and we do find it full.

2. In the first instance you will clearly see that there is a distinct plurality. The fishermen have nets—in the plural; they have boats—in the plural. There is plurality of agency employed. Each man seems to come out distinctly. In the next case, it is *one*. There are many men, but they are all in *one boat*. They unitedly drag the net, and it is but *one net*—there is no division, it is all one. Now, this is the visible and the invisible. To us, the means God makes use of to bring sinners to Himself are various.

Sometimes we are in one boat trying to catch all the fish we can. There is another boat over yonder, and they are trying to do the same. We ought to consider them as being partners, and whenever our boat gets too full, we should beckon to our partners in the other ship to come and help us. We ought not to look upon those brethren who differ from us as though they were emptying the sea, and rivaling us. The more the merrier. The more men to do good, the more will the Lord's name be praised.

I think, in many of our towns where some of our whining brethren say that all good people should go to one chapel, that it is far better to have three or four. I question whether the plurality of agency involved in denominations is not a great boon and blessing. Instead of, in the slightest degree, standing out against my brethren for carrying out their convictions, I praise them and look upon them as partners in another ship. Our denominational distinctions help to keep us awake; thus we stir one another up and do far more good in the world than would be the case if there were only a nominal church. God would have the agency diverse. There must be several nets, and there must be several fishermen, and these fishermen in different boats. So far as we are able to see, there will always be outward divisions in the ministry; and I avow myself the advocate and lover of these things. As I said last Sabbath, the thing called Sectarianism I do not disown but maintain.

But let us look to the inward. In John they are all in one boat, all fishing together, all dragging one net. Ah, brethren, this is what is really the fact. We do not see it, but all God's ministers are dragging one net, and all God's church is in one ship. Oh, I bless God for that sweet doctrine! It is no use striving after outward uniformity; we shall never see it. Neither the texture of the human mind nor the will of God require it. It is of no use to contend against the diversities which exist in the great visible church; I do not know that these differences are evils. They are the natural results of man's finite character, and must and will exist to the end of the chapter. It is the unity of the Spirit; it is unity in Christ Jesus; it is unity in love to one another that God would have us regard. Let us learn this unity from the fact, that after all, though we may look as if we differed, yet if we be God's ministers, there is only one fold and one shepherd. Though to our eyes it will always be so, two boats, or twenty boats; two nets, ay, fifty nets, yet to Him who sees all things better than we do, there is only one boat and one net; and they shall all who are taken in that one net be safely brought to shore.

3. There is another difference. In the first case, how many fish were caught? The text says, "a great multitude." In the second case, a great multitude are taken too, but they are all counted and numbered. "A hundred and fifty and three." Luke does not tell us how many were caught the first time, for there were some of them not worth the counting; but the second time you will perceive the exact number is recorded, "a hundred and fifty

and three." What was *Peter's* reason for counting them? We cannot tell. But I think I know why the Lord made him do it. It was to show us that though in the outward instrumentality of gathering the people into the church the number of the saved is to us a matter of which we know nothing definitely, yet secretly and invisibly the Lord has counted them even to the odd one, He knows well how many the gospel net shall bring in. See where the Word is preached what a great multitude are brought in! Thousands, tens of thousands are added to the different churches of Christ, and make a profession of their faith. It were impossible to reckon all over Christendom how many have been taken in the outward net of the visible Church of Christ. But, brethren, it is quite possible for it to be known of God how many shall be brought at last, and how many now are in the *invisible* church. He has counted them, foreordained their number, fixed them, settled them. The number "one hundred and fifty-three" seems to me to represent a large definite number. There shall be in heaven a number that no man can number, for God's elect are not few; but they shall be a number whom God can number, for "the Lord knoweth them that are his." They shall be a number certain and fixed, which shall neither be diminished nor increased, but still abide the same according to His purpose and will. Now, *I*, as a preacher, have nothing to do with counting fish. My business is with the great multitude. Splash goes the net again! Oh, Master! You who have taught us to throw the net and bring in a multitude, guide into it the hundred and fifty and three!

4. Yet again, notice another difference. The fish that were taken the first time appear to have been of all sorts. The net was broken and therefore, doubtless some of them got out again; there were some so little that they were not worth eating, and doubtless were thrown away. "They shall gather the good into vessels and throw the bad away." In the second case, the net was full of great fishes; they were all great fishes, all good for eating, all the one hundred and fifty-three were worth the keeping. There was not one little fellow to be thrown back into the deep again. The first gives us the outward and visible effect of the ministry. We gather into Christ's church a great number. And there will always be in that number some who are not good, that are not really called of God. Sometimes we have church-meetings in which we have to throw the bad away. We have many blissful meetings where it is gathering-in the fish—and what big hauls of fish has God given to us! Glory be to His name! But at other times we have to sit down and tell our fish over, and there are some who must be thrown away; neither God nor man can endure them. Thus is it in the outward and visible church. Let no man be surprised if the tares grow up with the wheat—it is the order of things, it must be so. Let none of us wonder if there be wolves in sheep's clothing—it always will be so. There was a Judas among the twelve; there will be deceivers among us to the end of the chapter. Not so

the invisible church—the church within the church—the holy of holies within the temple. In that there is none to throw away. No; the Lord who brought them into the net, brought the right sort in; He did not bring one hypocrite or apostate; and having brought them in to the exact number of one hundred and fifty and three, they cannot one of them get out again, but they are kept in that net, for that net does not break; they are in the secret invisible Church of Christ, and they cannot get out of it, let them do what they may. They may even give up their nominal profession, and thus get out of the visible church, but they cannot give up their secret possession; they cannot escape from the secret and invisible church, and they shall all be kept there till the net is dragged to land, and the whole 153 saved.

5. Yet again, you notice in the first case the net broke, and in the second case it did not. Now, in the first case, in the visible church the net breaks. My brethren are always calling out "the net is broken!" No doubt it is a bad thing for nets to break; but you need not wonder at it. We cannot just now, when the net is full, stop to mend it; it will break. It is the necessary consequence of our being what we are that the net will break. What mean you by this? Why, that instead of having some one denomination, we have twenty or thirty? The net is broken. I do not at all grieve over it. I believe it is what must be as long as we are flesh and blood. For until you get a set of perfect men, you never will have anything but these divisions. The net must break and will break. But glory be to God, the net does not break after all in reality, for though the visible church may seem to be rent and torn to pieces, the invisible church is one. God's chosen, God's called, God's quickened, God's blood-bought, they are one in heart, and one in soul, and one in spirit. Though they may wear different names among men, yet they still wear before God their Father's name written on their foreheads; and they are and always must be one.

You perceive, brethren, that I do not advise you to strive after a nominal unity. The more you strive after that, the more divisions there will be. Certain brethren left many of our denominations and formed, they said, a church that should not be a sect. All they did was to make a sect the most sectarian of sects—the most narrow and most bitter of cliques, though containing some of the best men, some of the best Christians, and the ablest writers of the times. You cannot make a visible uniformity, it is beyond your power—the net is broken.

There now! take care of the fish and leave the net alone, but still maintain the unity of the Spirit in the bond of perfectness. Take care that you are not a schismatic in your heart, that you hold no heresy in your soul, that you are one with all them that love the Lord Jesus Christ in sincerity; and in this you will soon see that the net is not broken, but that the saints are one. Ah, I bless God that when once we get with God's people—it does not matter what they are—we soon find the net is not broken. There is many a godly clergyman of the Church of England with whom I commune with the greatest joy, and I have found the net was not broken; and in conversing with brethren of all denominations, some who from doctrine, some who from sentiment stand wide as the poles asunder, I have still found and known that there was such a real and perfect harmony of heart that the net was not broken.

I do not believe that charity would ever have had such perfect work in Christ's church if it had not been for our being divided into tribes, like the twelve tribes of old. It is no charity for me to love a brother who thinks as I think—I cannot very well help it; but for me to love a dear brother who differs from me in some points, why there is exercise and room for my charity; and as God has left trials and troubles to exercise faith, I believe He has left us in many doctrinal difficulties on purpose to exercise our love till the day shall come when we shall all grow to the stature of perfect men in Christ Jesus. The net is not broken, brethren; do not believe it, and when you read about this denomination and that, do not be grieved at these names and tribes, but rather thank God for them; say, that is the visible church, and the net is broken; but there is an invisible church where the net is not broken, where we are one in Christ, and must be one forever.

There are several other points of difference, but I think we have hardly time to enlarge upon them. I will only hint at them. In the first case, which is the visible church, you see the human weakness becomes the strongest point; there is the boat ready to sink, there is the net broken, there is the men all out of heart, frightened, amazed and begging the Master to go away. In the other case it is not so at all. There is human weakness, but still they are made strong enough. They have no strength to spare, as you perceive, but still they are strong enough, the net does not break, the ship goes slowly to land dragging the fish; and then, lastly, Simon Peter pulls the fish to shore. Strong he must have been. They were just strong enough to get their fish to shore. So in the visible Church of Christ you will often have to mourn over human weakness: but in the invisible church, God will make His servants just strong enough—just strong enough to drag their fish to shore. The agencies, means, instrumentalities, shall have just sufficient force to land every elect soul in heaven, that God may be glorified.

Then, notice, in the first cast, in the visible church they launched out into the deep. In the second case, it says they were not far from the shore, but a little way. So today our preaching seems to us to be going out into the great stormy deep after fish. We appear to have a long way to reach before we shall bring these precious souls to land. But in the sight of God we are not far from shore; and when a soul is saved, it is not far from heaven. To us there are years of temptation, and trial, and conflict; but to God, the Most High, it is finished—"it is done." They are saved; they are not far from shore.

In the first case, the disciples had to forsake all and follow Christ. In the second, they sat down to feast with Him at the dainty banquet which He had spread. So in the visible church today we have to bear trial and self-denial for Christ, but glory be to God, the eye of faith perceives that we shall soon drag our net to land, and then the Master will say, "Come and dine"; and we shall sit down and feast in His presence, with Abraham, Isaac, and Jacob, in the kingdom of God.

One of the Lessons

My time is gone, and I close by noticing ONE OF THE LESSONS THE TWO NARRATIVES SEEM TO TEACH. In the first case, Christ was in the ship. Oh, blessed be God, Christ is in His church, though she launch out into the deep. In the second case, Christ was on the shore. Blessed be God, Christ is in heaven. He is not here, but He has risen; He has gone up on high for us. But whether He be in the church, or whether He be on the shore in heaven, *all our night's toiling shall, by His presence, have a rich reward.* That is the lesson. Mother, will you learn it? You have been toiling long for your children. It has been night with you as yet. They give no evidence of grace; rather they give many signs of sin, and they grieve your spirit. Your night's toiling shall have an end; you shall at last cast the net on the right side of the ship. Sunday school teacher, you have been diligently laboring long, and with but little fruit; do not be discouraged, the Master will not let you work in vain; in due season you shall reap if you faint not; and as these disciples had a great sea harvest, so shall you have a harvest of souls. Minister, you have been plowing some barren rock, and as yet no joyful sheaves have made your heart glad. You shall, doubtless, "Come again, rejoicing, bringing your sheaves with you." And you, O church of God, travailing for souls, meeting daily in prayer, pleading with men that they will come to Christ, what if they are not saved yet? The morning comes, the night is far spent, and the Master Himself shall soon appear; and though He may not find faith on the earth, yet His advent shall bring to His church the success for which she has waited—such success that as a woman remembers no more her travail because a man is born into the world, so shall the church remember no more her toils, her efforts on earth even as it is in heaven.

Work, dear friends! If there are any of you who are not working, *begin now.* If there are any of you not saved as yet, the Lord grant that when the Word is preached, you may be caught in it as in a net. We do throw it out once this morning; we hope to throw it again this evening. "Believe in the Lord Jesus Christ, and thou shalt be saved," for "he that believeth and is baptized shall be saved, and he that believeth not shall be damned." Flee to Christ! Escape from the wrath to come! May the Spirit apply that word to you, and lead you to the place where high on Calvary with bleeding hands and feet the Savior dies! One look at Him and you are saved. Look, sinner, and live! God save you, for Christ's sake! Amen.

6

*Christ Triumphant**

And having spoiled principalities and powers, he made a shew of them openly, triumphing over them in it (Colossians 2:15).

To the eye of reason the cross is the center of sorrow and the lowest depth of shame. Jesus dies a malefactor's death. He hangs upon the gibbet of a felon and pours out His blood upon the common mount of doom with thieves for His companions. In the midst of mockery, and jest, and scorn, and ribaldry, and blasphemy, He gives up the ghost. Earth rejects Him and lifts Him from her surface, and heaven affords Him no light but darkens the mid-day sun in the hour of His extremity. Deeper in woe than the Savior dived, imagination cannot descend. A blacker calumny than was cast on Him satanic malice itself could not invent.

He hid not His face from shame and spitting; and what shame and spitting it was! To the world the cross must ever be the emblem of shame, to the Jew a stumbling-block, and to the Greek foolishness. How different, however, is the view which presents itself to the eye of faith. Faith knows no shame in the cross, except the shame of those who nailed the Savior there; it sees no ground for scorn, but it hurls indignant scorn at sin, the enemy which pierced the Lord. Faith sees woe, indeed, but from this woe it marks a fount of mercy springing. It is true it mourns a dying Savior, but it beholds Him bringing life and immortality to light at the very moment when His soul was eclipsed in the shadow of death. Faith regards the cross, not as the emblem of shame, but as the token of glory.

The sons of Belial lay the cross in the dust, but the Christian makes a constellation of it, and sees it glittering in the seventh heaven. Man spits upon it, but believers, having angels for their companions, bow down and worship Him who ever lives though once He was crucified. My brethren, our text presents us with a portion of the view which faith is certain to discover when its eyes are anointed with the eye-salve of the Spirit. It tells us

* This sermon is taken from *The Metropolitan Tabernacle Pulpit* and was preached on Sunday morning, September 4, 1859.

that the cross was Jesus Christ's field of triumph. There He fought, and there He conquered, too. As a victor on the cross He divided the spoil. Nay, more than this; in our text the cross is spoken of as being Christ's triumphal chariot in which He rode when He led captivity captive, and received gifts for men.

Calvin thus admirably abounds the last sentence of our text: "The expression in the Greek allows, it is true, of our reading—*in Himself*; the connection of the passage, however, requires that we read it otherwise; for what would be meager as applied to Christ, suits admirably well as applied to the cross. For as He had previously compared the cross to a signal trophy or show of triumph, in which Christ led about His enemies, so He now also compares it to a triumphal car in which He showed Himself in great magnificence. For there is no tribunal so magnificent, no throne so stately, no show of triumph so distinguished, no chariot so elevated, as is the gibbet on which Christ has subdued death and the devil, the prince of death; nay, more, has utterly trodden them under His feet."

I shall today, by God's help, address you upon the two portions of the text. First, I shall endeavor to describe *Christ as spoiling His enemies on the cross*; and having done that I shall lead your imagination and your faith further on to see *the Savior in triumphal procession upon His cross*, leading His enemies captive, and making a show of them openly before the eyes of the astonished universe.

Christ Making a Spoil of Principalities and Powers

First, our faith is invited this morning to behold CHRIST MAKING A SPOIL OF PRINCIPALITIES AND POWERS. Satan, leagued with sin and death, had made this world the home of woe. The Prince of the power of the air, fell usurper, not content with his dominions in hell, must need invade this fair earth. He found our first parents in the midst of Eden. He tempted them to forego their allegiance to the King of heaven; and they became at once his bondslaves—bondslaves forever, if the Lord of heaven had not interposed to ransom them. The voice of mercy was heard while the fetters were being riveted upon their feet, crying, "*Ye shall yet be free*!" In the fullness of time there shall come One who shall bruise the serpent's head, and shall deliver his prisoners from the house of their bondage.

Long did the promise tarry. The earth groaned and travailed in its bondage. Man was Satan's slave, and heavy were the clanking chains which were upon his soul. At last, in the fullness of time, the Deliverer came forth born of a woman. This infant conqueror was but a span long. He lay in the manger—*He* who was one day to bind the old dragon and cast him into the bottomless pit, and set a seal upon him. When the old serpent knew that his enemy was born, he conspired to put Him to death; he leagued with Herod to seek the young child that he might destroy Him. But the providence of God preserved the future conqueror; He went down into Egypt, and there was He hidden for a little season. Anon, when He had come to fullness of years, He made His public advent, and began to preach liberty to the captives, and the opening of the prison to them that were bound.

Then Satan again shot forth His arrows, and sought to end the existence of the woman's seed. By divers means he sought to slay Him before His time. Once the Jews took up stones to stone Him; nor did they fail to repeat the attempt. They sought to cast Him down from the brow of a hill headlong. By all manner of devices they labored to take away His life, but His hour was not yet. Dangers might surround Him, but He was invulnerable till the time was come.

At last the tremendous day arrived. Foot to foot the conqueror must fight with the dread tyrant. A voice was heard in heaven, "This is your hour, and the power of darkness." And Christ Himself exclaimed, "Now is the crisis of this world; now must the prince of darkness be cast out." From the table of communion the Redeemer arose at midnight and marched forth to the battle. How dreadful was the contest! In the very first onset the mighty Conqueror seemed Himself to be vanquished. Beaten to the earth at the first assault, He fell upon His knees and cried, "My father, if it be possible let this cup pass from me." Revived in strength, made strong by heaven, He no longer quailed, and from this hour never did He utter a word which looked like renouncing the fight. From the terrible skirmish all red with bloody sweat, He dashed into the thick of the battle. The kiss of Judas was, as it were, the first sounding of the trumpet; Pilate's bar was the glittering of the spear; the cruel lash was the crossing of the swords. But the cross was the center of the battle; there, on the top of Calvary, must the dread fight of eternity be fought.

Now must the Son of God arise, and gird His sword upon His thigh. Dread defeat or glorious conquest awaits the Champion of the church. Which shall it be? We hold our breath with anxious suspense while the storm is raging. I hear the trumpet sound. The howlings and yells of hell rise in awful clamor. The pit is emptying out its legions. Terrible as lions, hungry as wolves, and black as night, the demons rush on in myriads. Satan's reserved forces, those who had long been kept against this day of terrible battle, are roaring from their dens. See how countless are their armies, and how fierce their countenances. Brandishing his sword the arch fiend leads the van, bidding his followers fight neither with small nor great, save only with the King of Israel.

Terrible are the leaders of the battle. Sin is there, and all its innumerable offspring, spitting forth the venom of asps, and infixing their poison-fangs in the Savior's flesh. Death is there upon his pale horse, and his cruel dart rends its way through the body of Jesus even to His inmost heart. He is "exceeding sorrowful, even unto death." Hell comes, with all its coals of juniper and fiery darts. But chief and head among them is Satan; remembering well the ancient day when Christ hurled him from the battlements of heaven, he rushes with all his malice yelling to the attack. The darts shot into the air are so countless that they blind the sun. Darkness covers the battlefield, and like that of Egypt it was a darkness which might be felt. Long does the battle seem to waver, for there is but one against many. One man—nay, tell it, lest any should misunderstand me, one *God* stands in battle array against ten thousands of principalities and powers. On, on they come, and He receives them all. Silently at first He permits their ranks to break upon Him, too terribly enduring hardness to spare a thought for shouting. But at last the battle-cry is heard. He who is fighting for His people begins to shout, but it is a shout which makes the church tremble.

He cries, "I thirst." The battle is so hot upon Him, and the dust so thick that He is choked with thirst. He cries, "I thirst." Surely, now, He is about to be defeated? Wait awhile; see yon heaps; all these have fallen beneath His arm, and as for the rest fear not the issue. The enemy is but rushing to his own destruction. In vain his fury and his rage, for see the last rank is charging, the battle of ages is almost over. At last the darkness is dispersed. Hark how the conqueror cries, "It is finished." And where are now His enemies? They are all dead. There lies the king of terrors, pierced through with one of his own darts! There lies Satan with his head all bleeding, broken! Yonder crawls the broken-backed serpent, writhing in ghastly misery! As for sin, it is cut in pieces, and scattered to the winds of heaven! "*It is finished*," cries the conqueror, as He came with dyed garments from Bozrah, "I have trodden the wine-press alone, I have trampled them in my fury, and their blood is sprinkled on my garments."

And now He proceeds to *divide the spoil.*

We pause here to remark that when the spoil is divided it is a sure token that the battle is completely won. The enemy will never allow the spoil to be divided among the conquerors as long as he has any strength remaining. We may gather from our text of a surety that Jesus Christ has totally routed, thoroughly defeated once for all, and put to retreat all His enemies, or else He would not have divided the spoil.

And now, what does this expression of Christ dividing the spoil mean? I take it that it means, first of all, that *He disarmed all His enemies.* Satan came against Christ; he had in his hand a sharp sword called the Law dipped in the poison of sin so that every wound which the law inflicted was deadly. Christ dashed this sword out of Satan's hand, and there stood the prince of darkness unarmed. His helmet was cleft in twain, and his head was crushed as with a rod of iron. Death rose against Christ. The Savior snatched his quiver from him, emptied out all his darts, cut them in two, gave Death back the feather end, but kept the poisoned barbs from him, that he might never destroy the ransomed. Sin came against Christ; but sin was utterly cut in pieces. It had been Satan's armor bearer, but its shield was cast away, and it lay dead upon the plain. Is it not a noble picture to behold all the enemies of Christ?—nay, my brethren, all your enemies, and mine, totally disarmed? Satan has nothing left him now wherewith he may attack us. He may attempt to injure us, but wound us he never can, for his sword and spear are utterly taken away. In the old battles, especially among the Romans, after the enemy had been overcome, it was the custom to take away all their weapons and ammunition; afterward they were stripped of their armor and their garments, their hands were tied behind their backs, and they were made to pass under the yoke. Now, even so has Christ done with sin, death, and hell; He has taken their armor, spoiled them of all their weapons, and made them all to pass under the yoke; so that now they are our slaves, and we in Christ are conquerors of them who were mightier than we.

I take it this is the first meaning of dividing the spoil—total disarming of the adversary.

In the next place, when the victors divide the spoil they carry away not only the weapons but all the treasures which belong to their enemies. They dismantle their fortresses and rifle all their stores, so that in the future they may not be able to renew the attack. Christ has done the like with all His enemies. Old Satan had taken away from us all our possessions. Paradise, Satan had added to his territories. All the joy, and happiness, and peace of man, Satan had taken—not that he could enjoy them himself, but that he delighted to thrust us down into povetry and damnation. Now, all our lost inheritances Christ has gotten back to us. Paradise is ours, and more than all the joy and happiness that Adam had, Christ has brought back to us. O robber of our race, how you are spoiled and carried away captive! Did you despoil Adam of his riches? The second Adam has stolen them from you! How is the hammer of the whole earth cut asunder and broken, and the waster is become desolate. Now shall the needy be remembered, and again shall the meek inherit the earth. "Then is the prey of a great spoil divided, the lame take the prey."

Moreover, when victors divide the spoil, it is usual to take away all the ornaments from the enemy, the crowns and the jewels. Christ on the cross did the like with Satan. Satan had a crown on his head, a haughty diadem of triumph. "I fought the first Adam," he said; "I overcame him, and here's my glittering diadem." Christ snatched it from his brow in the hour when He bruised the serpent's head. And now Satan cannot boast of a single victory, he is thoroughly defeated. In the first skirmish he vanquished manhood, but in the second battle manhood vanquished him. The crown is taken from Satan. He is no longer the prince of God's people. His reigning power is gone. He may tempt, but he cannot compel; he may threaten, but he cannot subdue; for the crown is taken from his head, and the mighty are brought low. O sing unto the Lord a new song, all you His people, make a joyful noise unto Him with psalms, all you His redeemed; for He has broken in sunder the gates of brass, and cut the bars of iron, He has broken the bow and cut the spear in sunder, He has burned the chariots in the fire, He has dashed in pieces our enemies, and divided the spoil with the strong.

And now, what does this say to us? Simply this. If Christ on the cross has spoiled Satan, let us not be afraid to encounter this great enemy of our souls. My brethren, in all things we must be made like unto Christ. We must bear our cross, and on that cross we must fight as He did with sin, and death and hell. Let us not fear. The result of the battle is certain, for as the Lord our Savior has overcome once even so shall we most surely conquer in Him. Be none of you afraid with sudden fear when the evil one comes upon you. If he accuse you, reply to him in these words: "Who shall lay anything to the charge of God's elect?" If he condemn you, laugh him to scorn, crying: "Who is he that condemns? It is Christ that died, yea rather hath risen again." If he threaten to divide you from Christ's love, encounter him with confidence: "I am persuaded that neither things present nor things to come, nor height nor depth, nor any other creature shall be able to separate us from the love of God which is in Christ Jesus our Lord." If he let loose your sins upon you dash the hell-dogs aside with this: "If any man sin *we* have an advocate with the Father, Jesus Christ the righteous." If death should threaten you, shout in his very face: "O grave! where is thy sting; O death! where is thy victory?"

Hold up the cross before you. Let that be your shield and buckler, and rest assured that as your master not only routed the foe but afterward took the spoil, it shall be even so with you. Your battles with Satan shall turn to your advantage. You shall become all the richer for your antagonists. The more numerous they shall be, the greater shall be your share of the spoil. Your tribulation shall work patience, and your patience experience, and your experience hope—a hope that makes you not ashamed. Through this much tribulation shall you inherit the kingdom, and by the very attacks of Satan shall you be helped the better to enjoy the rest which remains to the people of God. Put yourselves in array against sin and Satan. All you that bend the bow shoot at them, spare no arrows, for your enemies are rebels against God. Go up against them, put your feet upon their necks, fear not, neither be dismayed, for the battle is the Lord's and He will deliver them into your hands. Be very courageous, remembering that you have to fight with a stingless dragon. He may hiss, but his teeth are broken and his poison fang extracted. You have to do battle with an enemy already scarred by your Master's weapons. You have to fight with a naked enemy. Every blow you give him tells upon him, for he has nothing to protect him. Christ has stripped him naked, and divided his armor, and left him defenseless before His people. Be not afraid. The lion may howl, but rend you in pieces he never can. The enemy may rush in upon you with hideous noise and terrible alarms, but there is no real cause for fear. Stand fast in the Lord. You war against a king who has lost His crown; you fight against an enemy whose cheek-bones have been smitten, and the joints of whose loins have been loosed. Rejoice, rejoice in the day of battle, for it is for you but the beginning of an eternity of triumph.

I have thus endeavored to dwell upon the first part of the text, Christ on the cross divided the spoil, and He would have us do the same.

The Triumph of the Cross

The second part of our text refers not only to the dividing of the spoil, but to THE TRIUMPH. When a Roman general had performed great feats in a foreign country, his highest reward was that the senate should decree him a triumph. Of course there was a division of spoil made on the battlefield, and each soldier and each captain took his share; but every man looked forward rapturously to the day when they should enjoy the public triumph. On a certain set day the gates of Rome were thrown open; the houses were all decorated with ornaments; the people climbed to the tops of the houses, or stood in great crowds along the streets. The gates were opened, and by-and-by the first legion began to stream in with its banners flying, and its trumpets sounding. The people saw the stern warriors as they marched along the street returning from their blood-red fields of battle. After one half of the army had thus filed by, your eye would rest upon one who was the center of all attraction: riding in a noble chariot drawn by milk-white horses, there came the conqueror himself, crowned with the laurel crown and standing erect. Chained to his chariot were the kings and mighty men of the regions which he had conquered. Immediately behind them came part of the booty. There were carried the ivory and the ebony, and the beasts of the different countries which he had subdued. After these came the rest of the soldiery, a long stream of valiant men, all of them sharing the triumphs of their captain. Behind them came banners, the old flags which had floated aloft in the battle, the standards which had been taken from the enemy. And after these, large painted emblems of the great victories of the warrior. Upon one there would be a huge map depicting the rivers which he had crossed, or the seas through which his navy had found their way. Everything was represented in a picture, and the populace gave a fresh shout as they saw the memorial of each triumph. And then, behind, together with the trophies, would come the prisoners of less eminent rank. Then the rear would be closed with sound of trumpet, adding to the acclamation of the throng. It was a noble day for old Rome.

Children would never forget those triumphs; they would estimate their years from the time of one triumph to another. High holiday was kept. Women cast down flowers before the conqueror, and he was the true monarch of the day.

Now, our apostle had evidently seen such a triumph, or read of it, and he takes this as a representation of what Christ did on the cross. He says, "Jesus made a show of them openly, triumphing over them in it." Have you ever thought that the cross could be the scene of a triumph? Most of the old commentators can scarcely conceive it to be true. They say, "This must refer to Christ's resurrection and ascension. "Yes! while those hands were bleeding the acclamations of angels were being poured upon His head. Yes, while those feet were being pierced with the nails, the noblest spirits in the world were crowding around Him with admiration. And when upon that blood-stained cross He died in agonies unutterable, there was heard a shout such as never was heard before for the ransomed in heaven, and all the angels of God with loudest harmony chanted His praise. Then was sung, in fullest chorus, the song of Moses, the servant of God and of the Lamb, for He had indeed cut Rahab and sorely wounded the dragon. Sing unto the Lord, for He has triumphed gloriously. The Lord shall reign forever and ever, King of kings and Lord of lords.

I do not feel able, however, to work out a scene so grand, and yet so contrary to everything that flesh could guess as a picture of Christ actually triumphing on the cross—in the midst of His bleeding, His wounds, and His pains, actually being a triumphant victor, and admired of all. I choose, rather, to take my text thus: the cross is the ground of Christ's ultimate triumph. He may be said to have really triumphed there, because it was by that one act of His, that one offering of Himself, that He completely vanquished all His foes, and forever sat down at the right hand of the Majesty in the heavens. In the cross, to the spiritual eye, every victory of Christ is contained. It may not be there in fact, but it is there virtually; the germ of His glories may be discovered by the eye of faith in the agonies of the cross. Bear with me while I humbly attempt to depict the triumph which now results from the cross.

Christ has forever overcome all His foes and divided the spoil upon the battlefield, and now, even at this day is He enjoying the well-earned reward and triumph of His fearful struggle. Lift up your eyes to the battlements of heaven, the great metropolis of God. The pearly gates are wide open, and the city shines with her bejeweled walls like a bride prepared for her husband. Do you see the angels crowding to the battlements? Do you observe them on every mansion of the celestial city, eagerly desiring and looking for something which has not yet arrived? At last, there is heard the sound of a trumpet, and the angels hurry to the gates—the vanguard of the redeemed is approaching the city. Abel comes in alone, clothed in a crimson garb, the herald of a glorious army of martyrs. Hark to the shout of acclamation!

This is the first of Christ's warriors, at once a soldier and a trophy, that have been delivered. Close at his heels there follow others, who in those early times had learned the coming Savior's fame. Behind them a mighty host may be discovered of patriarchal veterans, who have witnessed to the coming of the Lord in a wanton age. See Enoch still walking with his God, and singing sweetly—"Behold the Lord cometh with ten thousands of His saints." There too is Noah, who had sailed in the ark with the Lord as his pilot. Then follow Abraham, Isaac, and Jacob, Moses, and Joshua, and Samuel, and David, all mighty men of valor. Hearken to them as they enter! Every one of them waving his helmet in the air, cries, "Unto him that loved us, and washed us from our sins in his blood, unto him be honor, and glory, and dominion, and power, forever and ever." Look, my brethren, with admiration upon this noble army!

Mark the heroes as they march along the golden streets, everywhere meeting an enthusiastic welcome from the angels who have kept their first estate. On, on they pour, those countless legions—was there ever such a spectacle? It is not the pageant of a day, but the "show" of all time. For four thousand years, on streams the army of Christ's redeemed. Sometimes there is a short rank, for the people have been often overcome and brought low; but, anon, a crowd succeeds, and on, on, still on they come, all shouting, all praising Him who loved them and gave Himself for them. But see, *He* comes! I see His immediate herald, clad in a garment of camel's hair, and a leathern girdle about his loins. The Prince of the house of David is not far behind. Let every eye be open. Now, mark, how not only angels, but the redeemed crowd the windows of heaven! He comes! He comes!

It is Christ Himself! Lash the snow-white coursers up the everlasting hills; "Lift up your heads, O ye gates, and be ye lifted up ye everlasting doors, that the King of glory may come in." See, He enters in the midst of acclamations. It is He! But He is not crowned with thorns. It is He! But though His hands wear the scar, they are stained with blood no longer. His eyes are as a flame of fire, and on His head are many crowns, and He has on His vesture and on His thigh written, KING OF KINGS AND LORD OF LORDS. He stands aloft in that chariot which is "paved with love for the daughters of Jerusalem." Clothed in a vesture dipped in blood, He stands confessed the emperor of heaven and earth.

On, on He rides, and louder than the noise of many waters and like great thunders are the acclamations which surround Him! See how John's vision is become a reality, for now we can see for ourselves and hear with our ears the new song, whereof He writes, "They sung a new song, saying, thou art worthy to take the book, and to open the seals thereof: for thou wast slain, and hast redeemed us to God by thy blood out of every kindred, and tongue, and people, and nation; and hast made us unto our God kings and priests: and we shall reign on the earth. And I beheld, and I heard the voice of many angels round about the throne and the beasts and the elders: and the number of them was ten thousand times ten thousand, and thousands of thousands; saying with a loud voice, worthy is the Lamb that was slain to receive power, and riches, and wisdom, and strength, and honor, and glory, and blessing. And every creature which is in heaven, and on the earth, and under the earth, and such as are in the sea, and all that are in them, heard I saying, blessing, and honor, and glory, and power, be unto him that sitteth upon the throne, and unto the Lamb forever and ever. And the four beasts said, amen. And the four and twenty elders fell down and worshiped him that liveth forever and ever."

But who are those at His chariot wheels? Who are those grim monsters that come howling in the rear? I know them. First of all there is the arch-enemy. Look to the old serpent, bound and fettered, how he writhes his ragged length along! His azure hues all tarnished with trailing in the dust, his scales despoiled of their once-vaunted brightness. Now is captivity led captive, and death and hell shall be cast into the lake of fire. With what derision is the chief of rebels regarded. How is he become the object of everlasting contempt. He who sits in the heavens laughs, the Lord has him in derision. Behold how the serpent's head is broken, and the dragon is trampled under foot. And now regard attentively yon hideous monster, *Sin*, chained hand in hand with his satanic sire. See how he rolls his fiery eye-balls, mark how he twists and writhes in agonies. Note how he glares upon the holy city, but is unable to spit his venom there, for he is chained and gagged, and dragged along an unwilling captive at the wheels of the victor. And there, too, is old Death, with his darts all broken and his hands behind him—the grim king of terrors, he too is a captive. Hark to the songs of the redeemed, of those who have entered into Paradise, as they see these mighty prisoners dragged along! "Worthy is he," they shout, "to live and reign at his Almighty Father's side, for he hath ascended upon on high, he hath led captivity captive, and received gifts for men."

And now behind Him I see the great mass of His people streaming in. The apostles first arrive in one goodly fellowship hymning their Lord; and then their immediate successors; and then a long array of those who through cruel mockings and blood, through flame and sword, have followed their Master. These are those of whom the world was not worthy, brightest among the stars of heaven. Regard also the mighty preachers and confessors of the faith: Chrysostom, Athanasius, Augustine, and the like. Witness their holy unanimity in praising their Lord. Then let your eye run along the glittering ranks till you come to the days of Reformation. I see in the midst of the squadron, Luther, and Calvin, and Zwingle, three holy brothers. I see just before them Wickliffe, and Huss, and Jerome of Prague, all marching together. And then I see a number that no man can number, converted to God through these mighty reformers, who now follow in the rear of the King of kings and Lord of lords. And looking down to our own time I see the stream broader and wider. For many are the soldiers who have in these last times entered into their Master's triumph. We may mourn their absence from *us*, but we must rejoice in their presence with the *Lord*. But what is the unanimous shout, what is the one song that still rolls from the first rank to the last? It is this: "Unto him that loved us, and washed us from our sins in his own blood, to him be glory and dominion forever and ever!" Have they changed the tune? Have they supplanted His name by another? Have they put the crown on another head, or elevated another hero into the chariot? Ah, no; they are content still to let the triumphant procession stream along its glorious length; still to rejoice as they behold fresh trophies of His love, for every soldier is a trophy, every warrior in Christ's army is another proof of His power to save, and His victory over death and hell.

I do not have time to enlarge further, or else I might describe the mighty pictures at the end of the procession; for in the old Roman triumphs, the deeds of the conqueror were all depicted in paintings. The towns he had taken, the rivers he had passed, the provinces he had subdued, the battles he had fought, were represented in pictures and exposed to the view of the people, who with great festivity and rejoicing, accompanied Him in throngs, or beheld Him from the windows of their houses, and filled the air with their acclamations and applause. I might present to you first of all the picture of hell's dungeons blown to atoms. Satan had prepared deep in the depths of darkness a prison-house for God's elect; but Christ has not left one stone upon another. On the picture I see the chains broken in pieces, the prison doors burned with fire, and all the depths of the vast deep shaken to their foundations. On another picture I see heaven open to all believers; I see the gates that were fast shut heaved open by the golden lever of Christ's atonement. I see another picture, the grave despoiled; I behold Jesus in it, slumbering for awhile, and then rolling away the stone and rising to immortality and glory.

But we cannot stay to describe these mighty pictures of the victories of His love. We know that the time shall come when the triumphant procession shall cease, when the last of His redeemed shall have entered into the city of happiness and of joy, and when with the shout of a trumpet heard for the last time, He shall ascend to heaven, and take His people up to reign with God, even our Father, forever and ever, world without end.

Our only question, and with that we conclude, is, have we a good hope through grace that we shall march in that tremendous procession? Shall we pass under review in that day of pomp and glory? Say, my soul, will you have an humble part in that glorious pageant? Will you follow at His chariot wheels? Will you join in the thundering hosannas? Shall your voice help to swell the everlasting chorus? Sometimes, I fear it shall not. There are times when the awful question comes—what if my name should be left out when He should read the muster-roll? Brethren, doesn't that thought trouble you? But yet I put the question again. Can you answer it? Will you be there—shall you see this pomp? Will you behold Him triumph over sin, death, and hell at last? Can you answer this question? There is another, but the answer will serve for both—do you believe on the Lord Jesus Christ? Is He your confidence and trust? Have you committed your soul to His keeping? Reposing on His might can you say for your immortal spirit—

> Other refuge have I none,
> Hangs my helpless soul on thee?

If you can say that, your eyes shall see Him in the day of His glory; nay, you shall share His glory, and sit with Him upon His throne, even as He has overcome and sits down with His Father upon His throne. I blush to preach as I have done today on a theme far beyond my power; yet I could not leave it unsung, but, as best I might, sing it. May God enlarge your faith, and strengthen your hope, and inflame your love, and make you ready to be made partakers of the inheritance of the saints in light, that when He shall come with flying clouds on wings of wind, you may be ready to meet Him, and may with Him ascend to gaze forever on the vision of His glory.

May God grant this blessing, for Christ's sake. Amen.

7

*Comfort from Christ's Omniscience**

Lord, thou knowest all things; thou knowest that I love thee (John 21:17).

Peter was somewhat hardly pressed. He felt that he was pushed into a corner, and compelled to look into his own heart, and divulge its innermost secret. To be asked once in the presence of his brethren whether he loved his Lord more than they did had a tendency to humiliate him, for he had boastfully declared that, though all men should be offended because of Christ, he would not. But to be asked, next, whether he really loved Christ at all, drove him to the ground with holy shame; and when his Master asked him the third time, "Simon, son of Jonas, lovest thou me?" Peter was grieved—not angry; that could not be his condition under such circumstances, nor was he rebellious. But, at last, his heart was effectually touched by his Master's skillful hand, and he was *grieved*, just as true love is always grieved when it is questioned, but most of all grieved when it is questioned again, and again, and again. Now, the enormity of his guilt in denying his Lord has come home to him, and the grief which he had caused his gracious Master is now reflected in his own deep and contrite sorrow: "Peter was grieved because he said unto him the third time, Lovest thou me?"

Our Savior's thus pressing him closely was no doubt necessary as a salutary discipline to Peter. It was not unkindness, but the highest form of honest tenderness which led our Lord to act in this way. I suppose that if such a thing had occurred in any one of our churches as for some leading member to deny that he knew Christ, and to go the length of denying it with oaths and curses, and to commit that great sin three times, in the pres-

* This sermon is taken from *The Metropolitan Tabernacle Pulpit* and was preached on Sunday evening, October 15, 1882.

ence of many witnesses, so that the fact could not possibly be doubted, it would have been absolutely necessary, according to the teaching of the New Testament, to exercise discipline upon such a man, and I think that he must have been excluded from church-fellowship.

The apostle Paul, writing concerning one who had been guilty of gross sin, says that, with such a man, we can have no fellowship—no, not so much as to eat with him; and he would have said the same about Peter. He had denied Christ with oaths and curses; it was a most heinous sin, and surely the purity of the church would be put in jeopardy—the very existence of the church as a testimony for Christ would be hazarded—by the retaining of such a man in its communion.

According to such a rule as that, I suppose we must always judge. But the Lord Jesus Christ possessed attributes which we have not; He was omniscient, and therefore He could read Peter's heart. It was not necessary for Him to do what it might be lawful and even needful for us to do. He knew that Peter's heart was right notwithstanding all the evil of which he had been guilty. So, instead of refusing to have fellowship with him, the Savior first eats with him—Christ literally bids him come to breakfast; and then He exercises what I may call a sort of church discipline upon him, though I mean that expression in no hard or unkind sense. Paul wrote to Timothy, "Then that sin rebuke before all, that others also may fear"; and our Lord acted in that manner on this occasion. The six other brethren, who might fitly be regarded as representing the entire church, were present; and the Savior began gently, but firmly, to probe Peter's heart, and to probe it again, and yet again, until He perceived that He had touched him in the most tender possible place, and had drawn from him this last and most solemn declaration of the sincerity of his love: "Lord, thou knowest all things; thou knowest that I love thee." Thrice had he denied his Lord; it was meet, therefore, that he should thrice confess his love, and so his Master constrained him to do by his thrice-repeated question, "Simon, son of Jonas, lovest thou me?"

Let us, dear friends, as we think over this sad incident of Peter's sin, and of our Lord's gracious way of restoring him to his former office by a gentle act of discipline, put ourselves through a little heart-searching. It may be that, thanks to the restraining grace of God, we have not sinned as Peter did; but we have sinned in some other way. We have all of us sinned quite enough to make us say, "Lord, do we love You?" Instead of waiting for Him to put the question to us, we will ask it of ourselves—Do we really and truly love the Lord? Let us also believe that our Lord, as He stands at this moment among us, and walks from pew to pew, bows His head over each one of us, and says, "Lovest thou me?"

As He does so, let us not evade the question, or play any tricks with it. Let not any one of us say, "I hope I do," or, "I am afraid I do not." We either do or we do not; and the only answer that will be satisfactory will be "Yes," or "No." If we say, "No," it will be so far satisfactory that we are speaking the truth; and, possibly, we may be helped to start back from so terrible a truth as that we do not love the Lord Jesus Christ, and that will be good for us, especially if it shall lead us to yield to Him. A man should always know the consequences of what he is doing, that he may do it with his eyes open; and, then, peradventure, he will see the folly and the sin of it, and take to a better course. But if, dear friend, you can answer, "Yes," to Christ's question, then do say it. Slowly, thoughtfully, as in the presence of the Eternal God, say, "Lord, I ask you to bear witness on my account, for your word is faithful and true: 'Thou knowest all things; thou knowest that I love thee.'" If you can say that, it will be a happy thing for yourself, and it will be a blessed thing for those who are around you. For now, being assured of your own love to Christ, you will endeavor to win others to share that love that many of you together may be able to say to Christ,

> Yes, we love Thee, and adore;
> Oh, for grace to love Thee more!

Now, coming to the text, I am going to try to do two things—first, to *examine Peter's reply*; and then, secondly, to *invite you to examine yourselves to see whether you can each give the same reply.*

Peter's Reply

First, let us EXAMINE PETER'S REPLY: "Lord, thou knowest all things; thou knowest that I love thee."

I begin with the observation that it is quite clear, from his reply, that *Peter was no Unitarian.* He had no doubts about the divinity of Christ, for he said to Him, "Lord, thou knowest all things." Now, there is no being conceivable as knowing all things except God; and if it be true that Jesus Christ knows all things, then He possesses omniscience which is one of the essential attributes of Deity. I find that, nowadays, there is a sad increase of that pestilent heresy which is practically a return to the old Arianism which sought to rob Christ of His true glory, and reduce Him to the level of a mere man. We, at any rate, are not tainted with that fatal error; God grant that we never may be! No; He who, as man, is our brother, is also God, our Lord and Savior, Jesus Christ, whom we worship and adore; and we think and speak of Him as possessing every attribute that is essential to the Deity, and, therefore, as possessing this one—that He knows all things. He searches the hearts and tries the reins of the children of men, for He is, assuredly, "very God of very God"; or, as Paul says, in his Epistle to the Romans, He "is over all, God blessed forever."

My next remark upon our text is that Peter's mention of omniscience in connection with Christ, and in connection with our declaration of love to

Him, may be regarded as *a fact very full of awe*, because the Christ with whom we have to deal knows everything of which we are thinking. He reads all that is in the very core and center of our soul. We are in the presence of One whose infinite knowledge takes in, at once glance, the whole of our lives—past, present, and future.

My dear friends, if we recollect that fact, it becomes a very solemn thing for us to make an appeal to Him to bear witness that we do really love Him. Peter said to Christ, "Lord, thou knowest all things," which in his case meant, "Lord thou knowest that, when the damsel said to me, 'Thou also wast with Jesus of Galilee,' I denied it, and said, 'I know not what thou sayest'; and when another maiden said, 'This fellow was also with Jesus of Nazareth,' I denied with an oath, and said, 'I do not know the man'; and then, as if to settle the matter once for all, and make my accusers believe that I could not be one of Christ's followers., I took to profane swearing, and with oaths and curses, like any son of Belial or lewd fellow of the streets, I did blaspheme and swear."

Yes, the Master had read the inner thoughts of Peter, as well as heard his words. Jesus knew all about how mean and cowardly he was to be afraid of a couple of silly maids, and of those who stood with the throng in the high priest's palace; yet Peter says, "Lord, thou knowest all things; thou knowest that I love thee."

As we think of poor Peter, and his answer to Christ's question, let us recollect that Jesus also knows everything that we have done since we were converted as well as before—all those times in which our thoughts have been impure and unclean, or our desires have wandered beyond the bounds of that which is right and proper, or our temper has been hasty and hot, or our spirit has been angry and proud. He sees the whole of our life in a single instant; God's mind does not need a certain space of time to think of one wrong thing which we have done, and then, afterward, to think of another; but it is all present before His eye at the same moment.

As when a man rises in a balloon, above London, and sees it all at once spread before Him, so God sees your life at the table, your life in the parlor, your life in the kitchen, your life in the workroom, your life in the bedchamber, your life everywhere—and, as you think of all that being under His immediate gaze, I think it must become a very solemn thing for you to say to Him, "Lord, thou knowest all this; and yet I dare call thee to witness that I do love thee notwithstanding all that thou hast seen."

Brothers and sisters, it is not by any means a trifling matter if our Lord only knows the sin of last week. Will you just think for a minute what it has been? Perhaps some of you may have grievously wronged the Savior during the week. If so, and remembering that He knows it all, can you yet creep up to Him, and say, "Lord, though I am fully conscious that You know all that has happened, yet, for all that, I do say, You also know that I love You." That is a fact full of awe.

It is, in the next place, *a fact which suggests to us that we should be very sincere*; for, if the Lord knows all things, then anything like an attempt to profess a love which we do not possess is utterly foolish, for God will search it through and through and discover its falseness. Then, in addition to being very foolish, it must be very wicked and insulting to the Lord. To tell another human being, whom you do not love, that you love him, would be a most cruel thing to do, and a most impudent and impertinent thing also; but voluntarily to express to God an affection which you do not feel is a very near approach to blasphemy. If it be not blasphemy in words, it certainly is in thought and intent.

God knows, friend, whether, when you joined the church, you were indeed a follower of Christ. That night, when you were baptized, he saw all that was done; and he knew exactly whether it was to you only an outward form, or whether you were really, in a spiritual sense, dead and buried with Christ. And when this service is over, it will be vain and futile for you to come to the communion table, and eat the bread, and drink of the cup, unless in your very soul you are trusting Christ, and believing in Him unto salvation. If you are determined to deceive someone, deceive your equal, play tricks with your fellow-creatures; but never think to deceive the Most High, who sees through you as if you were made of crystal, and at this moment is watching each beat of your heart, and reading not only what is on your tongue, but what is in your mind, and will come forth from your lips by-and-by.

Oh, let us never in our testimony talk beyond our own line or boast of virtues which we never possessed; and in our prayers, let us never pray as if we had an experience which we have never felt. But, let us say to Jesus, "Lord, thou knowest all things"; and let us be intensely sincere before Him; and it shall be a blessed thing if, being so, we then dare to say, "yet thou knowest that I love thee."

Further, dear friends, this is a fact which not only fills us with awe and suggests to us sincerity, but it is *a fact which inspires us with hope*. At times the grace that is really in us is scarcely visible to ourselves. I have often rejoiced that God's omniscience has enabled Him to spy out grace in me which I could not see, and I feel sure that there must be some of you who sometimes are led to question whether there is any grace in you or not. You ask, "Where is that grain of mustard seed?" Shame on you! Shame on you! You ought to have watered it till it grew into a tree. But remember that, even when you cannot see the grace that is in you, God can. When you are brought into such a state of diffidence and despondency that you are half afraid there is not any real love to Christ in your soul at all, yet, if it be there, He can see it, for He put it there; and He values it very highly, and has a quick eye to spy it out.

"Lord, You know all things; therefore, I do bless You that You know every place where I have been, and You know my secret love passages with You." That is a blessed thought. I have no doubt that, when Peter said to Christ, "Thou knowest all things," he not only recollected his sin, but he recollected his going out and weeping bitterly; and he also recollected the look that Jesus gave him—such a look as you and I could not give to anyone.

I do not know what Peter said to the Lord while he was weeping bitterly, but there must have been many a sigh, and many a groan, and many a tear, in that time of anguish. Peter no doubt got away into a corner, all alone, and he was ready to cover himself with sackcloth and ashes, as he there groaned, and wrestled, and cried. He did not know what to do with himself; and while he was thus praying, perhaps his Lord let in the light of the gospel, and made him recollect some such promise as this, "He that covereth his sins shall not prosper: but whoso confesseth and forsaketh them shall have mercy"; and Peter had some comfortable gleams of hope even amid the darkness, and, after a while, he did even dare to speak to his Lord, and tell Him he loved Him.

And now Peter says, "Lord, You know all things; You know that I love You, for between You and me there have been some love passages which nobody knows but You and me. My eyes, all full of tears, have met Your eyes all full of love; and my heart all breaking has touched Your heart which was pierced upon the tree. Your wounded hand has been laid to my sore, and Your weeping eyes have looked my tears away. You know, Lord; You know all things; You know that I love You." So, dear friends, you see that there is something exceedingly sweet about that omniscience which has read the secret motions of our spirit toward the Lord. Even when they have been so feeble that we could scarcely see them ourselves, God has seen them.

And do you not think, dear friends, that there is something very blessed in Peter's plan of bringing in Christ's omniscience to answer his Lord's question about his love, inasmuch as *it meets our inability to speak*? Some of us can speak fast enough, but others have the holy gift of silence, which is a great blessing. They cannot say much, but they can look up to their Savior and say, "Lord, You know all things; You know that we love You." I have heard of a young Christian woman, who was asked to tell before the church the story of her experience; but she could not utter a word, till, just as she was going out of the room, she turned round, and said, "I cannot speak for Jesus Christ, but I could die for Him." Then the one who was in charge of the meeting said to her, "Come back, dear sister, you have said quite enough for us to know that you love the Lord." No doubt there are many who find it easier to live for Christ than to speak for Him; they have not that gift. Let me remind you who must always be the silent members of the church, that you may be blessed in your silence by reflecting upon this fact, that God knows all about what you cannot explain to your fellow-Christians. His omniscience sets aside the necessity of your being able to express your love fluently, and you also can say, "Lord, You know all things; You know that we love You."

And is not this fact a *sweet encouragement to any of you who are persecuted for Christ's sake*? Our enemies do not burn us now, or stretch us on racks, but they have many methods of showing their malice still. They know how to torture us, and some of them are very ingenious in the art of tormenting. I have known some say—ungodly parents will say it to their daughters—sometimes, wicked men will say it to their gracious wives—"You know very well that all your idea about being religious is that you want to be singular. You go to your place of worship because you like to be different from everybody else; that is the only reason you have." Possibly, you do not know what to say to them; but you can always say this to your Savior, "Lord, You know all things; You know that I love You."

Then, again, if there is some little fault to be found with you in the family, down they come upon you, crying, "Ah! that is your Christianity, is it? You are one of those who have professed to be religious, and joined the church!" Mark you, friends, they will do a hundred times worse things themselves and think nothing of it; but if they can catch you tripping in the slightest degree, they magnify your little slip into a grievous fall. Now, it would be quite fair for them to do so if you set up to be perfect; but as you never did that, it is an unfair thing to charge you with insincerity because of imperfection. Do not let them have the opportunity of saying even that if you can help it; yet, sometimes, when you have given them no occasion for finding fault with you, they will make one and invent an accusation for which there is no foundation. Well, if they do so, never mind; let them say what they will, but lift up your eyes to heaven, and say, "Lord, You know all things; You know that I love You."

A man of God—as upright a Christian man as I know—came to me not long ago in great trouble because somebody had said that he had been drunk. He was dreadfully upset about it, for he had been a teetotaler for many years and nothing of the kind had occurred. "Well," I said, "you are only tarred with the same brush as others of us"; and then I added, "As for me, I have had all manner of false and cruel things said about me! I recollect that an influential daily paper said of me at the time of the Surrey Gardens accident, 'We would place, in the hand of every right-thinking man, a whip to scourge from society such a ranting charlatan.' Yet I am here still, notwithstanding all that was said. Moreover, when most abused, I used to go to bed at the same hour as I should have done with as hearty an appetite as if everybody had been praising me."

One gets by degrees into such a condition that it does not matter what people say. And, after all, does it ever really matter what they say? Let them throw mud at you till you are covered with it from head to foot; the kind of mud they fling has a tendency to come off when it is dry and to make the garment that it once sullied look even brighter than it was before. Do not fret yourselves about these slanderers and persecutors, but just get alone and say to the Lord, "'You know all things.' They do not; and it is a good thing for us that they do not. If they did, then they might find plenty of fault with us and find some real faults in us. But they do not know everything, and they generally hit on the very thing of which we are quite innocent; but, 'Lord, You know all things; You know that we love You.'"

This seems to me to be a blessed text for you to take home and to carry with you wherever you go in the midst of a ribald world, for *it will often remind you of a precious truth*: "You know all things; You know that I love You." Of course He does, if you do really love Him, for it is His own love in you returning whence it came, and He knows that it is there. If you do love Him, it was He who made you love Him. This plant of paradise never grows of its own accord in the dunghill of our nature; neither does it grow anywhere unless it is planted by the hand of God.

He who gave you that love watches over it to bring it to perfection. Being a plant of His own right-hand planting, He will water it every moment; and lest any hurt it, He will keep it night and day. Having loved the Lord here on earth, you shall love Him by-and-by in heaven, where, with all the blood-washed company, you shall find it the very heaven of your heaven to live forever, adoring Him whose eternal love, and sovereign grace, and almighty power have at last made you perfect and brought you home to love Him even as He loves you, according to your capacity.

Your Reply

There I must leave the text, so far as it specially concerns Peter, and come now to speak briefly upon the second part of the subject, which is, TO INVITE YOU TO EXAMINE YOURSELVES TO SEE WHETHER YOU CAN EACH GIVE THE SAME REPLY: "Lord, You know all things; You know that I love You."

First, *some say the same as Peter did, though they ought not to do so*. They say that they love Christ. "Yes, oh, yes; we love Him!" Let us talk to one of these glib speakers for a few moments. When did you begin to love the Lord? "Oh! I—I—I always did love Him." When were you converted, and renewed in heart? "Oh! I do not know that I ever was." Stop, then, friend, before you say again that you love the Lord. Do you truly trust the Savior? Are you resting the whole weight of your soul upon Him? If you say, "No," then you do not love Him, for the only love which Christ will accept is born of faith. Love is the flower which grows out of the root of faith.

Perhaps you think that you are very good, and that you will probably get to heaven by your goodness. If that is your notion, then I am sure you do not really love Christ. You admire your beautiful self; you have been so good, and so excellent, that you do not want to be saved by the sinners' Savior. You want a special, particular Savior for you—a saint-Savior, not a sinner's Savior. Then I know you do not love the Christ of the Bible—the Christ of Calvary. You may love a sort of antichrist of your own inventing, but you do not love the Christ of God. Let me ask you another question. You say that you love Christ; well, then, for what do you thank Christ? "Well, I believe that there are some imperfections in me, and that Christ makes up for them." Do you? Then, in your esteem, He is only a make-weight just to compensate for your deficiencies. His seamless robe of righteousness is to be torn to patch up your old rags!

How many of you want to make Christ a kind of extra horse to drag the load up the hill! That is all you think of Him; but do you imagine that Christ and your poor team are to be joined together like that? Is it to be partly self-salvation, and partly salvation by Christ? If that is your idea, you so insult the Savior—it may be unwittingly—that I am sure you cannot really love Him.

I have heard of a very excellent man—one of the holiest and best of men—who, when he lay dying, said, "Lord, when I estimate my works, I have to recollect that Your estimate is so very different from mine that I think it best to leave this business altogether, and trust my Savior only." I have heard of another who said, when he was dying, that he began to sort out his works, and some he thought were good, and some were bad; but after he had sorted them a little, he felt that the good ones were so very like the bad ones when he came really to look closely into them that he pitched the whole lot overboard, and just trusted himself to Christ. That was a very wise and sensible thing to do, and I am sure that no man among you loves Christ unless he is trusting to Him only, and to Him wholly.

What is your view of Christ, dear friend? Is he your Master as well as your Savior? This is a question which I want to put very pointedly, for I heard a person ask the other day, "Is baptism essential to salvation?" Listen. This man means to do only just that which is essential for his own salvation; that is all. To get into heaven is all that he cares about, so he asks concerning one thing or another, "Is it essential to salvation?"

A soldier in her Majesty's army says when an order is given to him, "Is this essential? Shall I be shot if I do not obey it?" Drum him out of the regiment, for what is the good of him?

I look upon Christ as my Lord and Master; and if He bids me do something, though there may be in it nothing whatever to my profit, I am bound to do it because He is my Master and Lord. "Is it essential to salvation?" is a sneak's question; I dare not use a milder term. I am often ashamed to answer those who make such an inquiry. The message to you is, "Whatsoever He says unto you, do it."

Did you come into the world merely that you might get saved? Is that all? Oh, poor, mean wretch! The Lord save you from being so selfish! How can you even get to heaven when your sole ambition is, somehow or other, to save your own skin? To get inside the pearly gates, and enjoy yourself—that is your notion of heaven; but that is the very thing from which you have to be saved. I hope you will come to Him who has saved me. I work, not because I hope to escape from hell by what I do, or to get to heaven by what I do, but because Christ has saved me; and now, out of gratitude to Him, if there is anything He wishes me to do, I do it without a question, saying to Him—

Hast thou a lamb in all the flock
  I would disdain to feed?
Hast thou a foe, before whose face
  I fear thy cause to plead?

Get rid of selfishness, or else you cannot truthfully say that you love Christ; you are only loving yourself and baptizing selfishness with the name of Christianity.

But, next, I think that *there are some persons who ought to say what Peter did, and yet they are afraid to do so.* Some of the most beautiful, tender, loving, genuine, true-hearted people in the world are, nevertheless, so timid and so jealous of themselves, and they have such brokenness of spirit, that they dare not say that they love Christ. Though I am sure that, if any people in the world do love Him, it is just these poor people. There are many who are so hard and harsh toward these dear tender, brokenhearted ones that I like to cheer them all I can. I wish that they would grow stronger; I wish that they would become bolder; I wish they were braver. But, then, I know that among these who dare not say publicly that they love Christ are many who love Him vastly better than some who can talk very glibly about it.

I have told you before of the two friends who were shut up in prison, and one said to the other, "Oh, I do dread tomorrow morning! I'm afraid that when I come to feel the fire, I shall recant. I know that I never was good at bearing pain, and I have heard that the pain of being burnt to death is very dreadful." So the other turned round upon him, and said, "I am ashamed of you talking like that; you know very well it is for Christ's cause that we are going to die. I am sure that I shall not have any such fear; I could bear a thousand deaths for Christ. I feel such courage in my spirit that I not dread the pain, and I am ashamed that you do."

They both came to be chained to the stake, and the boastful man recanted and saved his skin; but the poor timid man stood bravely in the midst of the fire, and burned to death, and kept only saying, "Lord, help me! Lord, help me!"

I believe that it often happens that those who are so trembling in themselves are, nevertheless, sound to the core. While many of your high-flying gentlemen, who get perfect in about three minutes and then begin to preach to those of us who have been, perhaps, thirty years in Christ, and tell us that we ought to be as perfect as they are—which we were before they were born—will be blown away like thistledown by the first wind that comes, and that the solid, weighty lumps of gold—these humble, brokenhearted saints—will endure even to the end.

Still, dear brother, where are you? Mr. Despondency, I mean. I want you to say, "Lord, You know all things; You know that I love You." Where are you, Mrs. Much-afraid? I think I have read about you in *Pilgrim's Progress*. Mrs. Much-afraid, and Mr. Despondency, and Mr. Feeble-mind, and Mr. Ready-to-halt, who had the crutches and went limping all his life; yet, once upon a time, when Mr. Great-heart cut off Giant Despair's head and brought it to the pilgrims, they said that they would all dance, and Ready-to-halt danced on his crutches and said that he hoped, by-and-by, to be where he should not be encumbered with them.

Come along, all you poor tried souls, let this be a time of rejoicing with you. Say in your spirit, if not in words, "Yes, Lord, we cannot hold back any longer, we must say it; 'You know all things; You know that we love You.'" And when you have once said it, keep on saying it, my dear brother or sister; and the Lord keep you up to that blessed mark till, when the trumpet sounds in the morning and you wake up in the endless day, you shall say, "Yes, Lord, I did love You, and I love You now, and I will love You forever." God grant that we may all say that for Christ's sake! Amen.

I will love Thee in life, I will love Thee in death,
And praise Thee as long as Thou lendest me breath;
And say, when the death-dew lies cold on my brow,
If ever I loved Thee, my Jesus, 'tis now.

8

*The Lord Is Risen Indeed**

Why seek ye the living among the dead? He is not here, but is risen: remember how he spake unto you when he was yet in Galilee (Luke 24:5,6).

The first day of the week commemorates the resurrection of Christ, and, following apostolic example, we have made the first day of the week to be our Sabbath. Does not this intimate to us that the rest of our souls is to be found in the resurrection of our Savior? Is it not true that a clear understanding of the rising again of our Lord is, through the power of the Holy Spirit, the very surest means of bringing our minds into peace? To have a part in the resurrection of Christ is to enjoy that Sabbath which remains for the people of God. We who have believed in the risen Lord do enter into rest, even as He also Himself is resting at the right hand of the Father. In Him we rest because His work is finished, His resurrection being the pledge that He has perfected all that is needful for the salvation of His people, and we are complete in Him. I trust that some restful thoughts may, by the power of the Holy Spirit, be sown in the minds of believers while we make a pilgrimage to the new tomb of Joseph of Arimathea and see the place where the Lord lay.

Instructive Memories

And, first, I will speak to you upon certain INSTRUCTIVE MEMORIES which gather around the place where Jesus slept "with the rich in his death." Though He is not there, He assuredly once was there, for "He was crucified, dead, and buried." He was as dead as the dead now are, and though He could see no corruption, nor could be held by the bands of death beyond the predestined time, yet He was in very deed most assuredly dead. No light remained in His eye, no life in His heart; thought had fled from His thorn-crowned brow, and speech from His golden mouth; He was not

* This sermon is taken from *The Metropolitan Tabernacle Pulpit* and was preached on Sunday morning, April 13, 1873.

in mere appearance, but in reality dead—the spear-thrust decided that question once for all; therefore in the sepulcher they laid Him, a dead man, fit occupant of the silent tomb. Yet as He is not there now, but is risen, it is for us to search for memorials of His having been there. Not for the "holy sepulcher" will we contend with superstitious sectaries, but in spirit we will gather up the precious relics of the risen Redeemer.

First, He has left in the grave *the spices*. When He rose He did not bring away the costly aromatics in which His body had been wrapped, but He left them there. Joseph brought about one hundred pounds of myrrh and aloes, and the odor remains still. In the sweetest spiritual sense, our Lord Jesus has filled the grave with fragrance. It no longer smells of corruption and foul decay, but we can sing with the poet of the sanctuary—

> Why should we tremble to convey
> These bodies to the tomb?
> There the dear flesh of Jesus lay,
> And left a long perfume.

Yonder lowly bed in the earth is now perfumed with costly spices and decked with sweet flowers, for on its pillow the truest Friend we have once laid His holy head. We will not start back with horror from the chambers of the dead, for the Lord Himself has traversed them, and where He goes no terror abides.

The Master also left his *graveclothes* behind Him. He did not come from the tomb wrapped about with a winding-sheet; He did not wear the elements of the tomb as the habiliments of life, but when Peter went into the sepulcher He saw the graveclothes lying carefully folded by themselves. What if I say He left them to be the hangings of the royal bedchamber wherein His saints fall asleep? See how He has curtained our last bed! Our dormitory is no longer bare and drear, like a prison cell, but hung around with fair white linen and comely drapes—a chamber fit for the repose of princes of the blood! We will go to our last bedchamber in peace, because Christ has furnished it for us.

Or if we change the metaphor, I may say that our Lord has left those graveclothes for us to look upon as pledges of His fellowship with us in our low estate, and reminders that as He has cast aside the death garments, even so shall we. He has risen from His couch and left His sleeping robes behind Him, in token that at our waking there are other vestures ready for us also.

What if I again change the figure and say that as we have seen old tattered flags hung up in cathedrals and other national buildings as the memorials of defeated enemies and victories won, so in the crypt where Jesus vanquished death His graveclothes are hung up as the trophies of His victory over death, and as assurances to us that all His people shall be more than conquerors through Him who loved them. "O death, where is thy sting? O grave, where is thy victory?"

Then, carefully folded up and laid by itself, our Lord left *the napkin* that was about His head. Yonder lies that napkin now. The Lord wanted it not when He came forth to life. You who mourn may use it as a handkerchief with which to dry your eyes. You widows and you fatherless children—you mourning brothers and you weeping sisters—and you, you Rachels, who will not be comforted because your children are not; here, take this which wrapped the Savior's face, and wipe your tears away forever. The Lord is risen indeed, and therefore thus says the Lord, "Refrain thy voice from weeping, and thine eyes from tears, for they shall come again from the land of the enemy," "Thy dead men shall live." O mourner—together, with the Lord's dead body, shall they arise; wherefore, sorrow not as they that are without hope, for if you believe that Jesus died and rose again, even so them also which sleep in Jesus will the Lord bring with Him.

> A cell where angels use
> To come and go with heavenly news.

Angels were not in the tomb before, but, at His resurrection they descended; one rolled away the stone, and others sat where the body of Jesus had lain. They were the personal attendants and bodyguard of the Great Prince, and therefore they attended Him at His rising, keeping the doorway, and answering the inquiries of His friends. Angels are full of life and vigor, but they did not hesitate to assemble at the grave, gracing the resurrection even as flowers adorn the spring. I do not read that our Master has ever recalled the angels from the sepulchers of His saints; and now, if believers die as poor as Lazarus, and as sick and as despised as he, angels shall convey their souls into the bosom of their Lord, and the bodies, too, shall be watched by guardian spirits, as surely as Michael kept the body of Moses and contended for it with the foe. Angels are both the servitors of living saints and the custodians of their dust.

What else did our Well-beloved leave behind Him? He left *an open passage* from the tomb, for the stone was rolled away—doorless is that house of death. We shall, in our turn, if the Master come not speedily, descend into the prison-house of the grave. What did I say?—I called it a "prison-house." But how a prison-house that has not bolts or bars—how a prison-house that has not even a door to close upon its occupants? Our Samson has pulled up the posts and carried away the gates of the grave with all their bars. The key is taken from the girdle of death and is held in the hand of the Prince of Life. The broken signal and the fainting watchmen are tokens that the dungeons of death can no more confine their captives.

As Peter, when He was visited by the angel, found his chains fall from off him while iron gates opened to him of their own accord, so shall the saints find ready escape at the resurrection morning. They shall sleep awhile, each one in his resting-place, but they shall rise readily, for the stone is rolled away. A mighty angel rolled away the stone, for it was very great, and when he had done the deed he sat down upon the stone. His garment was white as snow, and his face like lightning, and as he sat on the stone he seemed to say to death and hell, "Roll it back again if you can."

> Who shall rebuild for the tyrant his prison!
> The scepter lies broken that fell from his hands;
> His dominion is ended; the Lord is arisen;
> The helpless shall soon be released from their bands.

One other thing I venture to mention as left by my Lord in His forsaken tomb. I visited some few months ago several of the large columbaria which are to be found outside the gates of Rome. You enter a large square building sunk in the earth and descend by many steps, and as you descend you observe on the four sides of the great chamber innumerable little pigeonholes in which are the ashes of tens of thousands of departed persons. Usually in front of each compartment prepared for the reception of the ashes stands *a lamp*. I have seen hundreds, if not thousands, of these lamps, but they are all unlit, and indeed do not appear ever to have carried light; they shed no ray upon the darkness of death. But now our Lord has gone into the tomb and illuminated it with His presence, "the lamp of His love is our guide through the gloom." Jesus has brought life and immortality to light by the gospel; and now in the dovecotes where Christians nestle, there is light; yes, in every cemetery there is a light which shall burn through the watches of earth's night till the day break and the shadows flee away, and the resurrection morn shall dawn.

So then the empty tomb of the Savior leaves us many sweet reflections, which we will treasure up for our instruction.

Vain Searches

Our text expressly speaks of VAIN SEARCHES: "Why seek ye the living among the dead? He is not here, but is risen."

There are places where seekers after Jesus should not expect to find Him, however diligent may be their search, however sincere their desire. You cannot find a man where he is not, and there are some spots where Christ never will be discovered. At this present moment I see many searching for Christ among the monuments of *ceremonialism*, or what Paul called "the weak and beggarly elements," for they "observe days and months and times and years." Ever since our Lord arose Judaism and every form of symbolic ceremony have become nothing better than sepulchers. The types were of God's own ordaining, but when the substance had come, the types became empty sepulchers and nothing more. Since that time men have invented other symbols which have not even the sanction of Divine authority and are only dead men's graves.

At this present period the world has gone mad after its idols, deluded and deceived by those who have a zeal for God, but not according to knowledge. Surely there never was a period, even when Rome was most dominant, in which men heaped unto themselves ceremonies after such rate as at the present day. They have made Christianity to be a greater yoke of bondage than was Judaism itself; but in vain shall any sincere and awakened soul hope to find Jesus among these vain performances. You may stumble from one holy hocus-pocus to another, but you shall not find a Savior in any of them, for thus has He Himself declared, "Neither in this mountain nor yet at Jerusalem shall men worship the Father, but the hour cometh, and now is, when the true worshipers shall worship the Father in spirit and in truth, for the Father seeketh such to worship him."

Jesus has rent the veil and abolished ceremonial worship, and yet men seek to revive it, building up the sepulchers which the Lord has broken down. This day He repeats in our ears the warning, "Take ye good heed unto yourselves, for ye saw no manner of similitude on the day that the Lord spake unto you in Horeb out of the midst of the fire; lest ye corrupt yourselves, and make you a graven image, the similitude of any figure, the likeness of male and female." Yet certain men among us go about to set up the altars which our godly forefathers broke down, and the work of reformers and of Protestants must now be done over again. God send us a Knox or a Luther with a mighty hammer to break in pieces the idols which the priests of Baal are setting up! They seek the living among the dead. Jesus is not in their masses and processions. He is risen far above such carnal worship. If He were a dead Christ, such a worship might, perchance, be a suitable pageant over His tomb, but to one who ever lives, it must be insulting to present such materialistic service.

Alas! there are many others who are seeking Christ as their Savior among the tombs of *moral reformation*. Our Lord likened the Pharisees to white-washed sepulchers; inwardly they were full of dead men's bones, but outwardly they were fairly garnished. O, the way in which men when they get uneasy about their souls try to white-wash themselves. Some one gross sin is given up, not in heart, but only in appearance, and a certain virtue is cultivated not in the soul, but only in the outward act; and thus they hope to be saved, though they still remain enemies to God, lovers of sin, and greedy seekers after the wages of unrighteousness. They hope that the clean outside of the cup and the platter will satisfy the Most High and that He will not be so severe as to look within and try their hearts.

O sirs, why do you seek the living among the dead? Many have sought peace for their consciences by their moral reforms; but if the Holy Spirit has truly convinced them of sin, they have soon found that they were looking for a living Christ amidst the tombs. He is not here, for He is risen. If Christ were dead, we might well say to you, "Go and do your best to be your own saviors." But while Christ is alive, He wants no help of yours—He will save you from top to bottom, or not at all. He will be Alpha and Omega to you, and if you put your hand upon His work and think in any way that you can help Him, you have dishonored His holy name, and He will have nothing to do with you. Do not seek a living salvation amongst the sepulchers of outward formality.

Too many also are struggling to find the living Christ amidst the tombs which cluster so thickly at the foot of Sinai; for life they look to *the law*, whose ministry is death. They think that they are to be saved by keeping God's commandments. They are to do their best, and they conceive that their sincere endeavors will be accepted, and they will thus save themselves. This self-righteous idea is diametrically opposed to the whole spirit of the gospel. The gospel is not for you who can save yourselves, but for those who are lost. If you can save yourselves, go and do it, and do not mock the Savior with your hypocritical prayers. Go and stumble among the tombs of ancient Israel and perish as they did in the wilderness, for into rest Moses and the law can never lead you. The gospel is for sinners who cannot keep the law for themselves, who have broken it and incurred its penalty, who know that they have done so and confess it. For such, a living Savior has come that He may blot out their transgressions. Do not seek salvation by the works of the law, for by them shall no flesh living be justified. By the law is the knowledge of sin, and nothing more; but righteousness, peace, life, salvation come by faith in the living Lord Jesus Christ and by no other means. "Believe in the Lord Jesus Christ, and thou shalt be saved"; but if you try to establish your own righteousness, you shall surely perish because you have rejected the righteousness of Christ.

Others there are who seek the living Jesus among the tombs, by looking for something good in *human nature*, in their own natural hearts and dispositions. I can see you now, for I have known you long, and this has always been your folly, you will go into the charnel house of your own natures, and say, "Is Jesus here?" Beloved, you are sad and depressed, and I do not wonder. Look at yonder dry bones and bleaching skeletons. See that heap of rottenness, that mass of corruption, that body of death—can you bear it? "Ah," say you, "I am wretched indeed, but I long to find some good thing in my flesh!" O beloved, you sigh in vain, you might as well rake hell over to find heaven in it, as look into your own carnal nature to find consolation. Behold you this day, God has abandoned the old nature and given it up to death. Under the old law, circumcision was the putting away of the filth of the flesh, as though after this filth were gone the flesh might perhaps be bettered. But now, under the new covenant, we have a far deeper symbol, for "know ye not, that so many of us were baptized into Jesus Christ were baptized into his death? Therefore we are buried with him by baptism into death: that like as Christ was raised up from the dead by the glory of the Father, even so we also should walk in newness of life." The old man is buried, as a dead thing out of which no good can come. "Knowing this, that our old man is crucified with him, that the body of sin might be destroyed, that henceforth we should not serve sin." God does not attempt to renew the old carnal mind but to make us new creatures in Christ Jesus. If any man continually practices introspeculation with a view to consolation, he might as well pile up blocks of Wenham ice with a view to burn down a city. If you are turning over your frames and feelings, your thoughts and imaginations, to discover comfort, you might far sooner hope to find precious diamonds in the sweepings of the roads. "He is not here," says the whole of our old nature. He is not here, He is risen; and for consolation you must look alone to Him, as He is enthroned above the skies.

Yet again, too many have tried to find Christ amidst the gloomy catacombs of the world's *philosophy*. For instance, on the Lord's day they like to have a sermon full of thought—thought being in the modern meaning of it something beyond, if not opposite to, the simple teaching of the Bible. If a man tells his people what he finds in the Scriptures, he is said to "talk platitudes"; but if a man amuses his people with his own dreams, however opposed they may be to God's thoughts, he is a "thinking man," a "highly intellectual preacher." There be some who love above all things the maunderings of day-dreamers, and the crudities of skeptics. If they can hear what an infidel Professor has said against inspiration, if they can be indulged with the last new blasphemy, some hearers feel that they are making advances in that higher culture, which is so much vaunted now-a-days. But, believe me, the bat-haunted caves of false philosophy and pretended science have been searched again and again, but salvation dwells not in them.

In Paul's day there were Gnostics who tracked all the winding passages of vainglorious learning, but they only discovered "another gospel which was not another." The world by wisdom knew not God. After roaming amid the dreary catacombs of philosophy, we come back to breathe the fresh air of the living Word, and concerning the mazes of science, we gasp out the sentence—"He is not there." Reason has not found Him in her deepest mining, nor speculation in her highest soaring, though indeed He is not far from any one of us. Athens has her unknown God, but in the simple gospel God is known in the person of Jesus. Socrates and Plato hold up their candles, but Jesus is the sun. Our moderns argue and dispute, and yet a living Christ is among us converting sinners, cheering saints, and glorifying God. If the Lord were a dead question for debate, philosophy might help us; but as He is a living power, a grain of faith in Him is better than mountains of philosophy. O you who know not the inner life, and the quickening Spirit, what have you to do with the risen Lord? As well might corruption's worm become the judge of cherubim, as you become the arbiters of truth concerning Jesus our Lord.

How anxiously do I wish that you who have been searching for salvation in any of these directions would give up the hopeless task, and understand that Christ is nigh you, and if you with the heart believe on Him and with the mouth confess Him, you shall be saved. "Look unto me and be ye saved, all the ends of the earth; for I am God, and beside me there is none else": this is His cry to you. "Faith cometh by hearing, and hearing by the word of God." "Believe in the Lord Jesus Christ and thou shalt be saved," Jesus is living still and able to save to the uttermost. All you have to do is simply to turn the glance of your faith toward Him. By that faith He becomes yours, and you are saved, but seek not the living among the dead, for He is risen.

Unsuitable Abodes

We will again change our strain and consider, in the third place, UNSUITABLE ABODES. The angels said to the women, "He is not here, but is risen." As much as to say—since He is alive He does not abide here. The living Christ might have sat down in the tomb—He might have made the sepulcher His resting place, but it would not have been appropriate; and so He teaches us today that Christians should dwell in places appropriate to them. You are risen in Christ, you ought not to dwell in the grave. I shall now speak to those who, to all intents and purposes, live in the sepulcher though they are risen from the dead.

Some of these are excellent people, but their temperament, and perhaps their mistaken convictions of duty, lead them to be perpetually *gloomy and desponding*. They hope they have believed in Christ, but they are not sure; they trust that they are saved, but they would not be presumptuous enough to say so. They do not dare to be happy in the conviction that they are accepted in the Beloved. They love the mournful string of the harp, they mourn an absent God. They hope that the divine promises will be fulfilled: they trust that, perhaps, one of these days they may come forth into light, and see a little of the brightness of the Lord's love, but now they are ready to halt, they dwell in the valley of the shadow of death, and their soul is sore burdened.

Dear friend, do you think this is a proper condition for a Christian to be in? I am not going to deny your Christianity for a moment, for I have not half so much doubt about that as you have; I have a better opinion of you than you have of yourself. The most trembling believer in Jesus is saved, and your little faith will save you; but do you really think that Christ meant you to stay where you are, sitting in the cold and silent tomb, amid the dust and ashes? Why keep underground? Why not come into the Master's garden where the flowers are breathing perfume? Why not enjoy the fresh light of full assurance, and the sweet breath of the Spirit's comforting influences?

It was a madman who dwelt among the tombs, do not imitate him. Do not say I have been such a sinner that this is all I deserve to enjoy; for if you talk of deserving, you have left the gospel altogether. I know you believe in Jesus, and you would not give up your hope for all the world. You feel after all that He is a precious Christ to you; come, then, rejoice in Him, though you cannot rejoice in yourself. Come, beloved, come out of this dreary vault, leave it at once! Though you have lien among the pots, yet now shall you be as the wings of a dove covered with silver, and her feathers with yellow gold. Your Master comes to you now, and says, "O my dove, that art in the clefts of the rocks, in the secret places of the stairs, let me see Your countenance, let me hear Your voice; for sweet is Your voice, and Your countenance is comely."

Members of the body of a risen Savior, will you lie in the grave still? Arise and come away! Doubt no longer. O believer, what cause have you to doubt your God? Has He ever lied to you? Question no longer the power of the precious blood. Why should you doubt it? Is it not able to cleanse you from sin? No longer inquire as to whether you are saved or can be—if you believe you are as safe as Christ is. You can no more perish than Christ can if you are resting in Him—His word has pledged it, His honor is involved in it, He will surely bring you unto the promised rest; therefore be glad.

Why, I have known a brother who lived down in the catacombs and vaults so long that he has condemned his brethren for living in the sunlight, and has said, "I cannot understand a man speaking so confidently, I cannot understand it." My dear brother, because you cannot understand it, it is not therefore wrong. There is a great deal about eagles that owls do not understand. You who are always fretting and worrying in that way are sinning against God; you are grieving His Spirit; you are acting inconsistently with your Christian profession, and yet you judge others who believe God to be true and take Him at His word and, therefore, get joy and comfort out of His promise. Never do that, it would be wicked indeed for you to set yourselves up for judges.

Instead, pray the Lord to lift up the light of His countenance upon you, to give you joy and peace in believing, for this He says, "Rejoice in the Lord, you righteous, and shout for joy all you that are upright in heart." Come out of the tomb, dear brother, for Jesus is not here, and if He is not here why should you be? He is risen. O rise into comfort, too, in His Spirit's power.

Another sort of people seem to dwell among the tombs: I mean

Christians—and I trust real Christians—who are very *worldly*. It is no sin for a man to be diligent in business, but it is a grievous fault when diligence in business destroys fervency in spirit, and when there is no serving of God in daily life. A Christian man should be diligent so as to provide things honest in the sight of all men, but there be some who are not content with this. They have enough, but they covet more, and when they have more, they still stretch their arms like seas to grasp in all the shore, and their main thought is not God, but gold; not Christ, but wealth. O brethren, permit me earnestly to rebuke you, lest you receive a severe rebuke in providence in your own souls. Christ is not here! He dwells not in piles of silver. You may be very rich, and yet not find Christ in it all; and you might be poor, and yet if Christ were with you, you would be happy as the angels. He is not here, He is risen! A marble tomb could not hold Him, nor could a golden tomb have contained Him. Let it not contain you. Unwrap the cerements of your heart; cast all your care on God who cares for you. Let your conversation be in heaven. Set not your affection on things on the earth, but set it upon things above, where Christ sits at the right hand of God.

Once more on this point, a subject more grievous still, there are some professors who live in the dead-house of *sin*. Yet they say that they are Christ's people. Nay, I will not say they live in it, but they do what, perhaps, is worse—they go to sin to find their pleasures. I suppose we may judge of a man more by that wherein he finds his pleasure than by almost anything else. A man may say, "I do not habitually frequent the gaieties of the world; I am not always found where sin is mixed with mirth, and where worldlings dance upon the verge of hell, but I go there now and then for a special treat."

I cannot help quoting the remark of Rowland Hill, who, when he met with a professor who went to the theater, a member of his church, said to him, "I understand you attend the theater." "No," he said, "I only go for a treat now and then." "Ah," said Mr. Hill, "that makes it all the worse. Suppose that somebody said, 'Mr. Hill is a strange being, he eats carrion.' I am asked, 'Is it true, Mr. Hill, that you live on carrion?' 'No, I do not habitually eat carrion, but I have a dish of it now and then just for a treat.' Why, you would think I was nastier than I should have been if I had eaten it ordinarily."

There is much force in the remark. If anything that verges on the unclean and lascivious is a treat to you, why then your very heart is unclean, and you are seeking your pleasure and comfort among the dead. There are some things that men take pleasure in now-a-days that are only fit to make idiots laugh or else to cause angels to weep. Do be choice, Christian men and women, in your company. You are brothers to Christ; will you consort with the sons of Belial? You are heirs of perfection in

Christ, you are even now arrayed in spotless linen and are fair and lovely in the sight of God; you are a royal priesthood, the elect of mankind. Will you trail your garments in the mire and make yourselves the sport of the Philistines? Will you consort with the beggarly children of the world? No; act according to your pedigree and your newborn nature, and never seek the living among the dead.

Jesus was never there—go not there yourselves. He did not love the noise and turmoil of the world's pleasures; He had meat to eat of another kind. God grant you to feel the resurrection life strong within your spirits.

Unreasonable Services

But I pass on from that. In the fourth place, I want to warn you against UNREASONABLE SERVICES. Those good people to whom the angels said, "He is not here, but is risen," were bearing a load, and what were they carrying? What is Joanna carrying, and her servants, and Mary, what are they carrying? Why, white linen, and what else? Pounds of spices, the most precious they could buy. What are they going to do? Ah, if an angel could laugh, I should think he must have smiled as he found they were coming to embalm Christ. "Why He is not here: and, what is more, He is not dead, He does not want any embalming, He is alive." You might have seen all over England on Good Friday, and also on this Easter Sunday, crowds of people—I have no doubt very sincere people—and they hung crape over what they call their altars because He was dead and fasted and sang sad hymns over their dead Savior.

I bless the Lord my Redeemer is not dead, and I have no bells to toll for Him either. He is risen, He is not here! Here they come, crowds of them with their white linen, and their precious spices to wrap a dead Christ up in. Are the men mad? But they say, we were only acting it over again. Oh, was that it? Practical charades was it? Acting the glorious atonement of Calvary as a play! Then I accuse the performers of blasphemy before the throne of the eternal God who hears my words; I charge them with profanity in daring to rehearse in mimicry that which was once done and done forever and is never to be repeated.

No, I cannot suppose they meant to mimic the great sacrifice. Therefore, I conclude that they thought their Savior to be dead, and so they said, "Toll the bell for Him! Kneel down and weep before His image on a cross." If I believed Jesus Christ died on Good Friday, I would feast all day long because His death is over; as He has ordained the high festival of the Lord's Supper to be His commemoration, I would follow His bidding, and keep no fast. Who would sit down and whine over a friend once dead if you knew him to be restored to life and exalted in power? Why toll a bell for a living friend? However, I do not condemn the good people any more than the angels condemned those holy women. Only they may take their spices home and their white linen too, for Jesus is alive, and does not want them.

In other ways a great many fussy people do the same thing. See how they come forward in defense of the gospel. It has been discovered by geology and by arithmetic that Moses was wrong. Straightway many go out to defend Jesus Christ. They argue for the gospel, and apologize for it, as if it were now a little out of date, and we must try to bring it round to suit modern discoveries and the philosophies of the present period. That seems to me exactly like coming up with your linen and precious spices to wrap Him in. Take them away. I question whether Butler and Paley have not both of them created more infidels than they ever cured, and whether most of the defenses of the gospel are not sheer impertinences.

The gospel does not need defending. If Jesus Christ is not alive and cannot fight His own battles, then Christianity is in an evil case. But He is, and we have only to preach His gospel in all its naked simplicity, and the power that goes with it will be the evidence of its divinity. No other evidence will ever convince mankind. Apologies and defenses are well intended no doubt, so was the embalming well intended by these good women, but they are of small value. Give Christ room, give His preachers space and opportunities to preach the gospel, and let the truth be brought out in simple language, and you will soon hear the Master say, "Take away the spices, take away the linen! I am alive, I do not want these."

We see the same kind of thing in other good people who are sticklers for old-fashioned, stereotyped ways—they must have everything conducted exactly as it used to be conducted 100 or 200 years ago. Puritanic order must be maintained, and there must be no divergence. The way of putting the gospel must be exactly the same way in which it was put by good old Dr. So-and-so, and in the pulpit there must be the most awful dreariness that can possibly be compassed, and the preacher must be devoutly dull, and all the worship must be serenely proper—lots of spices and fine linen to wrap a dead Christ up in.

I delight to break down conventional proprieties. It is a grand thing to put one's foot right through merely human regulations, because life cannot be strapped down by regulations fit only for the dead. Death lies wrapped up like a mummy in the museum—it will always do the proper thing, or rather won't do anything at all; but life, real life, will show itself in unexpected ways. Life will say what death could not say, it will break out where it was not expected and break all your laws and regulations into a thousand pieces. But still I see the good people holding up their hands in horror, and crying out, "Bring hither the Arabian gum, the myrrh and the aloes, bring hither the linen, we must take care of our dear dead Master." Leave Him alone, leave Him alone, man, He is alive, and does not want your wrapping up.

I do not hesitate to say that a great deal of church order among Dissenters and Episcopalians, Presbyterians, and all sorts of sects, and a great deal of propriety and decorum, and regulation, and "As-it-was-in-the-beginning,-is-now,-and-ever-shall-be,"-ism are only so much spices and linen for a dead Christ, and Christ is alive, and what is wanted is to give Him room! I do not say this for my own sake—am I not always proper?—but I say it for the sake of earnest brother Evangelists who, in preaching to the poor, use extravagance of language, and perhaps of action. Let them use it. Gainsayers say they are histrionic. Was ever anybody ever half so histrionic as Ezekiel? Did not all the prophets do strange things to get the attention of the people? Why, the same charge was brought against Whitfield and Wesley—"These people are breaking through all rules," and so on. What a blessed thing it is when men can do it! Mr. Hill went to Scotland to preach the gospel, and they said he rode on the back of all order and decorum. Then said he, "I will call my pair of horses by those names, and make it true." It was true; no doubt, he did ride on the back of order and decorum. But then he drew souls to Christ with those two strange steeds, and his breaking through rules enabled him to get at men and women who never would have been reached in any other way. Be ready to set Christ at liberty and give His servants liberty to serve Him as the Spirit of God shall guide them.

The Amazing News

I wanted to speak, last of all, upon THE AMAZING NEWS which these good women received: "He is not here, but he is risen." This was amazing news to His enemies. They said, "We have killed Him—we have put Him in the tomb; it is all over with Him." A-ha! Scribe, Pharisee, Priest, what have you done? Your work is all undone, for He is risen! It was amazing news for Satan. He no doubt dreamed that he had destroyed the Savior, but He is risen! What a thrill went through all the regions of hell! What news it was for the grave! Now it was utterly destroyed, and death had lost his sting!

What news it was for trembling saints. "He is risen indeed." They plucked up courage, and they said, "The good cause is the right one still, and it will conquer, for our Christ is still alive at its head. It was good news for sinners. Ay, it is good news for every sinner here. Christ is alive; if you seek Him, He will be found of you. He is not a dead Christ to whom I point you today. He is risen; and He is able to save to the uttermost those who come unto God by Him. There is no better news for sad men, for distressed, desponding, and despairing men, than this—the Savior lives, able still to save and willing to receive you to His tender heart. This was glad news, beloved, for all the angels and all the spirits in heaven, glad news indeed for them. And this day it shall be glad news to us, and we will live in the power of it by the help of His Spirit. We will tell it to our brethren that they may rejoice with us, and we will not despair any longer. We will give way no more to doubts and fears, but we will say to one another, "He is risen indeed; therefore let our hearts be glad." The Lord bless you, and in coming to His table, as I trust many of His people will come, let us meet our risen Master. Amen.

9

*Resurrection with Christ**

But God, who is rich in mercy, for his great love wherewith he loved us, even when we were dead in sins, hath quickened us together with Christ, (by grace ye are saved) (Ephesians 2:4,5).

There have been conferences of late of all sorts of people upon all kinds of subjects, but what a remarkable thing a conference would be if it were possible of persons who have been raised from the dead! If you could somehow or other get together the daughter of the Shunammite, the daughter of Jairus, the son of the widow at the gates of Nain, Lazarus, and Eutychus, what strange communings they might have one with another! What singular inquiries they might make, and what remarkable disclosures might they present to us! The thing is not possible, and yet a better and more remarkable assembly may be readily gathered on the same conditions, and more important information may be obtained from the confessions of its members. This morning we have a conference of that very character gathered in this house; for many of us were dead in trespasses and sins, even as others, but we hope that through the divine energy we have been quickened from the spiritual death and are now the living to praise God. It will be well for us to talk together, to review the past, to rejoice in the present, to look forward to the future. "You hath he quickened who were dead in trespasses and sins"; and as you sit together, an assembly of men possessed of resurrection life, you are a more notable conclave than if merely your bodies and not your spirits had been quickened.

The first part of this morning's discourse will be occupied with *a solemnity in which we shall take you into the charnel house*; secondly, we shall spend awhile in *reviewing a miracle*, and *we shall observe dead men living*; we shall then turn aside to observe *a sympathy indicated* in the text; and we shall close with a *song*, for the text reads somewhat like music—

* This sermon is taken from *The Metropolitan Tabernacle Pulpit* and was preached on Sunday morning, April 12, 1868.

it is full of thankfulness, and thankfulness is the essence of true song; it is full of holy and adoring wonder; it is evermore true poetry even though expressed in prose.

Solemnity

Celebrate first a great SOLEMNITY and descend into the charnel house of our poor humanity. According to the teaching of sacred Scripture, men are dead, spiritually dead. Certain vain men would make it out that men are only a little disordered and bruised by the fall, wounded in a few delicate members, but not mortally injured. However, the Word of God is very express upon the matter, and declares our race to be not wounded, not hurt merely, but slain outright and left as dead in trespasses and sin.

There are those who fancy that fallen human nature is only in a sort of syncope of fainting fit, and only needs a process of reviving to set it right. You have only, by education and by other manipulations, to set its life-floods in motion, and to excite within it some degree of action, and then life will speedily be developed. There is much good in every man, they say, and you have only to bring it out by training and example. This fiction is exactly opposite to the teaching of sacred Scripture. Within these truthful pages, we read of no fainting fit, no temporary paralysis, but death is the name for nature's condition, and quickening is its great necessity. Man is not partly dead like the half-drowned mariner in whom some spark of life may yet remain, if it be but fondly tendered and wisely nurtured. There is not a spark of spiritual life left in man—manhood is to all spiritual things an absolute corpse. "In the day thou eatest thereof thou shalt surely die," said God to our first parents, and die they did—a spiritual death. All their children alike by nature lie in this spiritual death—not a sham death, or a metaphorical one, but a real, absolute, spiritual death.

Yet it will be said, "Are they not alive?" Truly so, but not spiritually. There are grades of life. You come first upon the vegetable life; but the vegetable is a dead thing as to the vitality of the animal. Above the animal life rises the mental life, a vastly superior life; the creature, which is only an animal, is dead to either the joys or the sorrows of mental life. Then, high above the mental, as much as the mental is above animal, rises what Scripture calls the spiritual life—the life in Christ Jesus. All men have more or less of the mental life, and it is well that they should cultivate it—get as much as they can of it, that they should put it to the best uses, and make it subserve the highest ends. Man, even looked upon as merely living mentally, is not to be despised or trifled with. But still the mental life cannot of itself rise above the spiritual life, it cannot penetrate beyond that mystic wall which separates forever the mere life of mind from the life of that new principle, the Spirit, which is the offspring of God, and is the living and incorruptible which He casts into the soul.

If you could conceive a man in all respects like yourselves, with this one difference, that his soul had died out of him, that he only possessed his animal faculties but had no intellectual faculties, so that he could breathe and walk, sleep and eat, and drink, and make a noise, but all mental power was gone, you would then speak of him as being entirely dead to mental pursuits. He might be a most vigorous and well-developed animal, but his manhood would be dead. It would be of no use explaining a proposition to him, or working out a problem on the blackboard for his instruction, or offering him even the simplest schoolbook, for if he had no mind to receive, how could he impart?

Now, spiritually, this is the condition of every unregenerate man. It is of no use whatever, apart from the Spirit of God, to hope to make the man understand spiritual things, for they are spiritually discerned, says the apostle. The carnal mind cannot understand the things of God—when best trained it has no glimmering of the inward sense of spiritual things; it stumbles over the letter and loses the real meaning, not from want of mental capacity, but from the absence of spiritual life. O sons of men, if you would know God, "You must be born again"; "Except a man be born again, he *cannot* see the kingdom of God," he cannot understand it, he cannot know it. The carnal man cannot understand the things which are of God, which are eternal and invisible, any more than an ox can understand astronomy or a fish can admire the classics. Not in a moral sense, nor a mental sense, but in a spiritual sense, poor humanity is dead, and so the Word of God again and again most positively describes it.

Step with me, then, into the sepulcher-house, and what do you observe of yonder bodies which are slumbering there? They are quite unconscious? Whatever goes on around them, neither occasions them joy nor causes them grief. The dead in their graves may be marched over by triumphant armies, but they shout not with them that triumph. Or, friends they have left behind may sit there, and water the grass upon the green mound with their tears, but no responsive sigh comes from the gloomy cavern of the tomb. It is thus with men spiritually dead: they are unaffected by spiritual things. A dying Savior, whose groans might move the very adamant, and make the rocks dissolve, they can hear of all unmoved. Even the all-present Spirit is undiscerned by them, and His power unrecognized. Angels, holy men, godly exercises, devout aspirations, all these are beyond and above their world. The pangs of hell do not alarm them, and the joys of heaven do not entice them. They hear after a sort mentally, but the spirit-ear is fast shut up, and they do not hear. They are unconscious of all things which are of a spiritual character: eyes have they, but they see not, and ears, but they hear not.

You can interest them in the facts of geology, or the discoveries of art, but you cannot win their hearts to spiritual emotions and pursuits because they are as unaware of their meaning as an oyster of whelk is unacquainted with the disestablishment of the Irish church. Carnal men blunder over the first words of spiritual knowledge as Nicodemus did who, when he was told that he must be born again, began to inquire, "How can a man be born again when he is old?" or, like the woman of Samaria, who, when she was told of the living water, could not understand the spiritual truth and exclaimed in wonder, "Thou hast nothing to draw with, and the well is deep: from whence then hast thou that living water?" Men are spiritually unconscious of spiritual truth, and so far dead to it.

Observe that corpse: you may strike it, you may bruise it, but it will not cry out; you may pile burdens upon it, but it is not weary; you may shut it up in darkness, but it feels not the gloom. So the unconverted man is laden with the load of his sin, but he is not weary of it; he is shut up in the prison of God's justice, but he does not long for liberty; he is under the curse of God, as it is written, "Cursed is every one that continueth not in all things which are written in the book of the law to do them," but that curse causes no commotion in his spirit because he is dead. Well may some of you be peaceful because you are not aware of the terrors which surround you.

A man totally deaf is not startled by thunder-claps; if totally blind, he is not alarmed by the flashing of the lightning. He does not fear the tempest which he does not discern. Even thus is it with you who are at ease in your sins, you cannot discern the danger of your sin, you do not perceive the terror that rises out of it, else let me tell you there were no sleep to those wanton eyes, no rest to those giddy spirits; you would cry out in grief the very moment you received life, nor would you rest till delivered from those evils which now ensure for you a sure damnation. Oh! were you but alive, you would never be quiet till you were saved from the wrath to come. Man remains unconscious of spiritual things, and unmoved by them because, in a spiritual sense, he is dead.

Invite yonder corpse to assist you in the most necessary works of philanthropy. The pestilence is abroad, ask the buried one to kneel with you and invoke the power of heaven to recall the direful messenger; or, if he prefers it, ask him to assist you in purifying the air and attending to sanitary arrangements. You ask in vain, however needful or simple the act he cannot help you in it. And in spiritual things, it is even so with the graceless. The carnal man can put himself into the posture of prayer, but he cannot pray; he can open his mouth and make sweet sounds in earthborn music, but to true praise he is an utter stranger. Even repentance, that soft and gentle grace which ought to be natural to the sinful, is quite beyond his reach.

How shall he repent of a sin the weight of which he cannot feel? How shall he pray for a blessing the value of which he has no power to perceive? How shall he praise a God in whom he feels no interest, and in whose existence he takes no delight? I say that to all spiritual things the man is quite as unable as the dead are unable to the natural works and services of daily life.

"And yet," says one, "we heard you last Lord's day tell these dead people to repent and be converted." I know you did, and you shall hear me yet again do the like. But why speak to the dead thus and tell them to perform actions which they cannot do? Because my Master bids me, and as I obey my Master's errand, a power goes forth with the word spoken, and the dead start in their sleep and wake through the quickening power of the Holy Spirit. They who naturally cannot repent and believe, *do* repent and believe in Jesus and escape from their former sins and live. Yet, believe me, it is no power of theirs which makes them thus start from their death-sleep, and no power of mine which arrests the guilty, slumbering conscience—it is a power divine which God has yoked with the Word which He has given forth when it is fully and faithfully preached.

Therefore have we exercised ourselves in our daily calling of bidding dead men live because life comes at the divine bidding. But dead they are, most thoroughly so, and the longer we live the more we feel it to be so. The more closely we review our own condition before conversion, and the more studiously we look into our own condition even now, the more fully do we know that man is dead in sin, and life is a gift—a gift from heaven, a gift of undeserved love and sovereign grace, so that the living must everyone of them praise God and not themselves.

One of the saddest reflections about poor dead human nature is what it will be. Death in itself, though a solemn matter, is not so dreadful as that which comes of it. Many a time when that dear corpse has first been forsaken of the soul, those who have lost a dear one have tried to imprint that cold brow with kisses still. The countenance has looked even more lovely than in life, and when friends have taken the last glimpse, there has been nothing revolting, but much that was attractive. Our dead ones have smiled like sleeping angels, even when we were about to commit them to the grave. Ah! but we cannot shake from us a wretched sense of what is sure to be revealed before long. It is only a matter of time and corruption must set in. It must bring with it its daughter putridity, and by-and-by, the whole must be so noxious that if you had kept it above ground so long you would vehemently cry with Abraham, "Bury my dead out of my sight!" for the natural and inevitable result of death is corruption. So it is with us all. Some are manifestly corrupt, ah, how soon! While yet they are youths we see them plunging into infamous vice. They are corrupt in the tongue with lying words and lascivious speaking; corrupt in the eye with wanton glances; corrupt certainly at heart, and then corrupt thoroughly in life.

There are many about us in the streets every day the stink of whose corruption compels us to put them out of society for we are very decent; even those who are dead themselves are very scrupulous not to associate with those who are too far gone in corruption. The dead bury their dead and roll the stone and put away the debauched and dissolute. We do not ask the rotten sinners into our households because they might corrupt us too fast; and we flatter ourselves that we are so much superior, whereas they are only a stage or two ahead in a race which all unregenerate men are running. This corruption, though not developed in all to the same extent visibly, will be plain enough at the last in another world. When God finds us dead, He will cast us out where the worm does not die and the fire is not quenched.

What will be the development of an unregenerate character in hell I cannot tell, but I am certain it will be something which my imagination dares not now attempt to depict, for all the restraints of this life which have kept men decent and moral will be gone when they come into the next world of sin. As heaven is to be the perfection of the saint's holiness, so hell will be the perfection of the sinner's loathsomeness, and there will he discover, and others will discover, what sin is when it comes to its worst. "When lust hath conceived, it bringeth forth sin: and sin, when it is finished, bringeth forth death"; and this, dear hearer, do we solemnly remind you will be your portion forever and ever, unless God be pleased to quicken you.

Unless you be made to live together with Christ you will be in this world dead, perhaps in this world corrupt, but certainly so in the next world, where all the dreadful influences of sin will be developed and discovered to the very fullest. And you shall be cast away from the presence of God and the glory of His power. There can be no death in heaven, neither can corruption inherit incorruption. If you have not been renewed in the spirit of your mind, within those pearly gates you can never have your portion, and where the light of heaven shines in perpetual noonday your lot can never be cast. Weigh these thoughts, I pray you; if they are not according to this book reject them. But as they most certainly are, refuse them at your peril, but rather let them take possession of your careful spirit and lead you to seek and find eternal life in Christ Jesus the Lord.

A Miracle

We now change the subject for something more pleasant, I observe A MIRACLE, or *dead men made alive.*

The great object of the gospel of Christ is to create men anew in Christ Jesus. It aims at resurrection and accomplishes it. The gospel did not come into this world merely to restrain the passions or educate the principles of men, but to infuse into them a new life which, as fallen men, they did not possess. I saw yesterday what seemed to me a picture of those preachers whose sole end and aim is the moralizing of their hearers, but who have not learned the need of supernatural life.

Not far from the shore were a dozen or more boats at sea dragging for two dead bodies. They were using their lines and grappling irons and, what with hard rowing and industrious sailing, were doing their best most commendably to fish up the lost ones from the pitiless sea. I do not know if they were successful, but if so, what further could they do with them but decently to commit them to their mother earth?

The process of education and everything else, apart from the Holy Spirit, is a dragging for dead men, to lay them out decently side by side in the order and decency of death, but nothing more can man do for man. The gospel of Jesus Christ has a far higher task: it does not deny the value of the moralist's efforts or decry the results of education; but it asks what more can you do, and the response is, "Nothing." Then it bids the bearers of the bier stand away and make room for Jesus, at whose voice the dead arise. The preacher of the gospel cannot be satisfied with what is done in drawing men out of the sea of outward sin. He longs to see the lost life restored; he desires to have breathed into them a new and superior life to what they have possessed before.

Go your way, education, do your best, you are useful in your sphere; go your way, teacher of morality, do your best, you too are useful in your own manner. But if it comes to what man really needs for eternity, you, all put together, are little worth—the gospel, and the gospel alone, answers to men's requirements: man must be regenerated, quickened, made new, have fresh breath from heaven breathed into him or the work of saving him is not begun. The text tells us that God has done this for His people, for those who trust in Him. Let us observe the dry bones as they stir and stand before the Lord, and observing, let us praise the Lord that, according to His great love wherewith He loved us, He has quickened us together with Christ.

In this idea of quickening, there is a *mystery*. What is that invisible something which quickens a man? Who can unveil the secret? Who can track life to its hidden fountain? Brother, you are a living child of God—what made you live? You know that it was by the power of the Holy Spirit. In the language of the text, you trace it to God, you believe your new life to be of divine implantation. You are a believer in the supernatural; you believe that God has visited you as He has not visited other men and has breathed into you life. You believe rightly, but you cannot explain it.

We know not of the wind from whence it comes or whither it goes, so is everyone who is born of the Spirit. He who should sit down deliberately and attempt to explain regeneration and the source of it might sit there till he grew into a marble statue before he would accomplish the task. The Holy Spirit enters into us, and we who were dead before to spiritual things begin to live by His power and indwelling. He is the great worker, but how the Holy Spirit works is a secret that must be reserved for God Himself. We need not wish to understand the mode; it is enough for us if we partake of the result.

It is a great mystery then; but, while it is a mystery, it is a great *reality*. We know and do testify, and we have a right to be believed, for we trust we have not forfeited our characters, that we are now possessors of a life which we knew nothing of some years ago, that we have come to exist in a new world, and that the appearance of all things outside of us is totally changed from what it used to be. "Old things have passed away, behold all things are become new." I bear witness that I am this day the subject of sorrows which were no sorrows to me before I knew the Lord, and that I am uplifted with joys which I should have laughed at the very thought of if anyone had whispered the name of them in my ears before the life divine had quickened me.

This is the witness of hundreds of us, and although others disbelieve us, they have no right to deny our consciousness because they have not partaken of the like. If they have never tried it, what should they know about it? If there should be an assembly of blind men, and one of them should have his eyes opened and begin to talk of what he saw, I can imagine the blind ones all saying, "What a fool that man is! There are no such things." "Here I have lived in this world seventy years," says one, "and I never saw that thing which he calls a color, and I do not believe in his absurd nonsense about scarlet and violet, and black and white; it is all foolery together." Another wiseacre declares, "I have been up and down the world and all over it for forty years, and I declare I never had the remotest conception of blue or green, nor had my father before me. He was a right good soul and always stood up for the grand old darkness. 'Give me,' said he, 'a good stick and a sensible dog, and all your nonsensical notions about stars, and suns, and moons, I leave to fools who like them.'"

The blind man has not come into the world of light and color, and the unregenerate man has not come into that world of spirit. Hence, neither of them is capable of judging correctly.

I sat one day, at a public dinner, opposite a gentleman of the gourmand species, who seemed a man of vast erudition as to wines and spirits and all the viands of the table; he judged and criticized at such a rate that I thought he ought to have been employed by our provision merchants as taster in general. He had finely developed lips, and he smacked them frequently. His palate was in a fine critical condition. He was also as proficient in the quantity as in the quality and disposed of meats and drinks in a most wholesale manner. His retreating forehead, empurpled nose, and protruding lips made him, while eating at least, more like an animal than a man. At last, hearing a little conversation around him upon religious matters, he opened his small eyes and his great mouth and delivered himself of this sage utterance, "I have lived sixty years in this world, and I never felt or believed in anything spiritual in all my life."

The speech was a needless diversion of his energies from the roast duck. We did not want him to tell us that. I, for one, was quite clear about it before he spoke. If the cat under the table had suddenly jumped on a chair and said the same thing, I should have attached as much importance to the utterance of the one as to the declaration of the other; and so, by one sin in one man and another in another man, they betray their spiritual death.

Until a man has received the divine life, his remarks thereon, even if he be an archbishop, go for nothing. He knows nothing about it according to his own testimony. Then why should he go on to try to beat down with sneers and sarcasms those who solemnly avow that they have such a life, and that this life has become real to them, so real that the mental life is made to sink into a subordinate condition compared with the spiritual life which reigns within the soul?

This life brings with it the *exercise of renewed faculties.* The man who begins to live unto God has powers now which he never had before: the power really to pray, the power heartily to praise, the power actually to commune with God, the power to see God, to talk with God, the power to receive tidings from the invisible world, and the power to send messages up through the veil which hides the unseen up to the very throne of God. Now, the man instead of dreading God and betaking himself to some outward form, ceremony, or other outward way of pushing God further off, puts away his ceremonies, casts away the beggarly elements which once might have pleased him, and draws near to his God in spirit, and speaks to Him. "Father," says he, and God owns the kindred. I wish we all possessed this life, and I pray if we have it not that God may send it to us, for if we have it not the testimony of the word is that we are dead when most we seem to be alive.

I shall not, however, keep you longer upon this quickening except to say that you may easily image to yourself the inward experience of a man who received new life from the dead. You may conceive it by the following picture. Suppose a man to have been dead and to have been buried like others in some great necropolis, some city of the dead, in the catacombs. An angel visits him, and by mercy's touch he lives. Now, can you conceive that man's first emotion when he begins to breathe? There he is in the coffin—he feels stifled, pent up. He had been there twenty hears, but he never felt inconvenienced until now. He was easy enough, in his narrow cell, if ease can be where life is not. The moment he lives he feels a horrible sense of suffocation. Life will not endure to be so hideously compressed, and he begins to struggle for release. He lifts with all his might that dreadful coffin lid! What a relief when the decaying plank yields to his pressure!

So the ungodly man is content enough in his sin, his Sabbath-breaking, his covetousness, his worldliness, but the moment God quickens him his sin is as a sepulcher to the living. He feels unutterably wretched; he is not in a congenial position; and he struggles to escape. Often at the first effort the great black lid of blasphemy flies off, never to be replaced. Satan thought it was screwed down fast enough, and so it was for a dead man, but life makes short work of it and many other iniquities follow.

But to return to our resurrection in the vault: the man gasps a minute and feels refreshed with such air as the catacomb affords him; but soon he has a sense of clammy damp about him, and feels faint and ready to expire. So the renewed man at first feels little but his inability and groans after power. He cries, "I want to repent; I want to believe in Jesus; I want to be saved." Poor wretch! He never felt that before—of course he did not—he was dead; now he is alive, and hence he longs for the tokens, signs, fruits, and refreshments of life.

Do you not see our poor friend who has newly risen? He has slipped down from that niche in the wall where they laid him, and finding himself in a dark vault, he rubs his eyes to know whether he really is alive or whether it is all a dream. It is such a new thing. As by the little glimmering of light that comes in, he detects hundreds of others lying in the last sleep and says to himself, "Great God! What a horrible place for a living man to be in! Can I be myself alive?" He begins to wander about searching for a door by which he may escape. He loathes those winding sheets in which they wrapped him; he begins stripping them off; they are damp and mildewed; they do not suit a living man. Anon, he cries out; perhaps there is some passer-by who may hear him, and he may be delivered from his confinement. So a man who has been renewed by grace, when he partly discovers where he is, cries out, "This is no place for me."

That giddy ballroom—why, it was well enough for one who knew no better. That saloon was suitable for an unregenerate soul—but what can an heir of heaven do in such places? Lord, deliver me. Give me light and liberty. Bring my soul out of prison that I may live and praise Your name. The man pines for liberty; and if, at last, he stumbles to the door of the vault and reaches the open air, I think he drinks deep draughts of the blessed oxygen! How glad he is to look upon the green fields and the fresh flowers. You do not imagine that he will wish to return to the vaults again; he will utterly forsake those gloomy abodes. He shudders at the remembrance of the past, and would not for all the world undergo again what he has once passed through. He is tenderly affected at every remembrance of the past and is especially fearful lest there should be others like himself newly quickened who may need a brother's hand to set them at liberty. He loathes the place where once he slept so quietly.

So the converted man dreads the thought of going back to the joys which once so thoroughly fascinated him. "No," says he, "they are no joys to me. They were joys well enough for my old state of existence. But now, having entered into a new life, a new world, they are no more joys to me than the spade and shroud are joys to a living man. I can only think of them with grief and of my deliverance with gratitude."

Sympathy

I must pass on very briefly to the third point. The text indicates A SYMPATHY: "He hath quickened us *together with Christ.*" What does that mean? It means that the life which lives in a saved man is the same life which dwells in Christ. To put it simply—when Elisha had been buried for some years, we read that they threw a man who was dead into the tomb where the bones of Elisha were, and no sooner did the corpse touch the prophet's bones than it lived at once. Yonder is the cross of Christ, and no sooner does the soul touch the crucified Savior than it lives at once, for the Father has given to Him to have life in Himself and life to communicate to others. Whosoever trusts Christ has touched Him, and by touching Him he has received the virtue of eternal life—to trust in the Savior of the world is to be quickened through Him.

We are quickened together with Christ in three senses: First, *representatively.* Christ represents us before the eternal throne; He is the second Adam to His people. So long as the first Adam lived the race lived, and so long as the second Adam lives the race represented by Him lives before God. Christ is accepted, believers are accepted; Christ is justified, the saints are justified; Christ lives, and the saints enjoy a life which is hid with Christ in God.

Next we live by *union* with Christ. So long as the head is alive the members have life. Unless a member can be severed from the head and the body maimed, it must live so long as there is life in the head. So long as Jesus lives, every soul that is vitally united to Him, and is a member of His body, lives according to our Lord's own word, "Because I live ye shall live also." Poor Martha was much surprised that Christ should raise her brother from the dead. But He said, as if to surprise her still more, "Whosoever liveth and believeth in me shall never die. Believest thou this?" This is one of the things we are to believe, that when we have received the spiritual life, it is in union with the life of Christ and consequently can never die. Because Christ lives, our life must abide in us forever.

Then we also live together with Christ as to *likeness.* We are guickened together with Christ, that is, in the same manner. Now, Christ's quickening was in this wise. He was dead through the law, but the law has no more dominion over Him now that He lives again. So you, Christian, you are cursed by the old law of Sinai, but it has no power to curse you now for you are risen in Christ. You are not under the law; its terrors and threatenings have nothing to do with you. Of our Lord it is written, "In that he liveth," it is said, "he liveth unto God." Christ's life is a life unto God. Such is yours. You are not henceforth to live unto the flesh to mind the things of it; but God who gave you life is to be the great object of your life—*in* Him you live, and *for* Him you live. Moreover, it is said, "Christ being raised from the dead dieth no more; death has no more dominion over Him." In that same way the Christian lives; he shall never go back to his spiritual death—having once received divine life, he shall never lose it. God does not play fast and loose with His chosen; He does not save today, and damn tomorrow. He does not quicken us with the inward life and then leave us to perish; grace is a living, incorruptible seed, which lives and abides forever. "The water that I shall give Him," says Jesus, "shall be in him a well of water springing up unto everlasting life." Glory be to God, then, you who live by faith in Christ, live an immortal life, a life dedicated to God, a life of deliverance from the bondage of the law; rejoice in it, and give your God all the praise!

Brethren and sisters, if you have indeed been thus made alive as others are not, you have first of all, in the language of the text, to praise *the great love* of God, great beyond all precedent. It was love which made Him breathe into Adam the breath of life and make poor clay to walk and speak; but it is far greater love which makes Him now, after the fall has defiled us, renew us with a second and yet higher life. He might have made new creatures by millions out of nothing. He had but to speak, and angels would have thronged the air, or, beings like ourselves, only pure and unfallen, would have been multiplied by myriads upon the greensward.

If He had left us to sink to hell as fallen angels had done before us, who could have impugned His justice? But His great love would not let Him leave His elect to perish. He loved His people, and therefore, He would cause them to be born again. His great love wherewith He loved us defied death, and hell, and sin. Dwell on the theme you who have partaken of this love! He loved *us*, the most unworthy, who had no right to such love. There was nothing in us to love, and yet He loved us, loved us when we were dead. Here His great love seems to swell and rise to mountainous dimensions: love to miserable sinners, love to loathsome sinners, love to the dead and to the corrupt. O, heights and depths of sovereign grace, where are the notes which can sufficiently sound forth your praise? Sing, O redeemed, of His great love wherewith He loved us, even when we were dead in sins.

And do not cease to praise God as you think of the riches of His mercy, for we are told that He is rich in mercy, rich in His nature as to mercy, rich in His covenant as to treasured mercy, rich in the person of His dear Son as to purchased mercy, rich in providential mercy, but richest of all in the mercy which saves the soul. Friends, explore the mines of Jehovah's wealth if you can. Take the key and open the granaries of your God, and see the stores of love which He has laid up for you. Strike your sweetest notes to the praise of God, who is rich in mercy, for His great love wherewith He has loved us.

And let the last note and the highest and the loudest of your songs be that with which the text concludes, "By grace are ye saved." O never stammer there; brethren and sisters, whatever you do hold or do not hold, never be slow to say this, "If saved at all, I am saved by grace; grace in contradistinction to human merit, for I have no merit; grace in contradistinction to my free will, for my own free will would have led me further and further from God. Preventing grace brought me near to Him." Do bless and magnify the grace of God, and as you owe all to it cry, "Perish each thought of pride," consecrate yourself entirely to the God to whom you owe everything. Desire to help to spread the savor of that grace which has brought such good things to you. And vow in the name of the quickening Spirit that He who has made you live by faith shall from this day till you enter into heaven have the best of your thoughts, and your words, and your actions, for you are not your own. You have been quickened from the dead, and you must live in newness of life. The Lord bless you, dear friends; if you have never spiritually lived, may He give you grace to believe in Jesus this day, and then you are alive from the dead. And if you are alive already, may He quicken you yet more and more by His eternal Spirit, till He brings you to the land of the living on the other side of the Jordan. Amen.

10

Following the Risen Christ[*]

If ye then be risen with Christ, seek those things which are above, where Christ sitteth on the right hand of God. Set your affection on things above, not on things on the earth (Colossians 3:1,2).

The resurrection of our divine Lord from the dead is the cornerstone of Christian doctrine. Perhaps I might more accurately call it the keystone of the arch of Christianity, for if that fact could be disproved the whole fabric of the gospel would fall to the ground.

"If Jesus Christ be not risen then is our preaching vain, and your faith is also vain; ye are yet in your sins." If Christ be not risen, then they which have fallen asleep in Christ have perished; and we ourselves, in missing so glorious a hope as that of resurrection, are of all men the most miserable.

Because of the great importance of His resurrection, our Lord was pleased to give many infallible proofs of it by appearing again and again in the midst of His followers. It would be interesting to search out how many times He appeared; I think we have mention of some sixteen manifestations. He showed Himself openly before His disciples, and did eat and drink with them. They touched His hands and His side, and heard His voice, and knew that it was the same Jesus who was crucified. He was not content with giving evidence to the ears and to the eyes, but even to the sense of touch He proved the reality of His resurrection.

These appearances were extremely varied. Sometimes He gave an interview to one alone, either to a man, as to Cephas, or to a woman, as to Magdalene. He conversed with two of His followers as they went to Emmaus and with the company of the apostles by the sea. We find Him at one moment among the eleven when the doors were shut for fear of the Jews, and at another time in the midst of an assembly of more than 500 brethren, who years after were most of them living witnesses to the fact. They could not all have been deceived. It is not possible that any histori-

* This sermon is taken from *The Metropolitan Tabernacle Pulpit* and was preached on Sunday morning, March 28, 1880.

cal fact could have been placed upon a better basis of credibility than the resurrection of our Lord from the dead. This is put beyond all dispute and question, and of purpose is it so done, because it is essential to the whole Christian system.

For this same cause the resurrection of Christ is commemorated frequently. There is no ordinance in Scripture of any one Lord's-day in the year being set apart to commemorate the rising of Christ from the dead, for this reason, that every Lord's-day is the memorial of our Lord's resurrection. Wake up any Lord's-day you please, whether in the depth of winter or in the warmth of summer, and you may sing—

Today He rose and left the dead,
  And Satan's empire fell;
Today the saints His triumph spread,
  And all His wonders tell.

To set apart an Easter Sunday for special memory of the resurrection is a human device, for which there is no scriptural command; but to make every Lord's-day an Easter Sunday is due to Him who rose early on the first day of the week. We gather together on the first rather than upon the seventh day of the week because redemption is even a greater work than creation, and more worthy of commemoration, and because the rest which followed creation is far outdone by that which ensues upon the completion of redemption. Like the apostles, we meet on the first day of the week, and hope that Jesus may stand in our midst, and say, "Peace be unto you." Our Lord has lifted the Sabbath from the old and rusted hinges whereon the law had placed it long before, and set it on the new golden hinges which His love has fashioned. He has placed our restday, not at the end of a week of toil, but at the beginning of the rest which remains for the people of God. Every first day of the week we should meditate upon the rising of our Lord, and seek to enter into fellowship with Him in His risen life.

Never let us forget that all who are in Him rose from the dead in His rising. Next in importance to the fact of the resurrection is the doctrine of the federal headship of Christ, and the unity of all His people with Him. It is because we are in Christ that we become partakers of everything that Christ did—we are circumcised with Him, dead with Him, buried with Him, risen with Him, because we cannot be separated from Him. We are members of His body and not a bone of Him can be broken. Because that union is most intimate, continuous, and indissoluble, therefore all that concerns Him concerns us, and as He rose so all His people have arisen in Him.

They are risen in two ways. First, representatively. All the elect rose in Christ in the day when He quitted the tomb. He was justified, or declared to be clear of all liabilities on account of our sins, by being set free from the prison-house of the tomb. There was no reason for detaining Him in the sepulcher, for He had discharged the debts of His people by dying "unto sin once." He was our hostage and our representative; and when He came forth from His bonds, we came forth in Him. We have lain in its prison and even died under its death-warrant, and now we are no longer under its curse. "Now if we be dead with Christ, we believe that we shall also live with him: knowing that Christ being raised from the dead dieth no more; death hath no more dominion over him. For in that he died, he died unto sin once; but in that he liveth, he liveth unto God."

Next to this representative resurrection comes our spiritual resurrection, which is ours as soon as we are led by faith to believe in Jesus Christ. Then it may be said of us, "And you hath he quickened who were dead in trepasses and sins."

The resurrection blessing is to be perfected by-and-by at the appearing of our Lord and Savior, for then our bodies shall rise again, if we fall asleep before His coming. He redeemed our humanity in its entirety, spirit, soul, and body, and He will not be content until the resurrection which has passed upon our spirit shall pass upon our body too. These dry bones shall live; together with His dead body they shall rise.

> When He arose ascending high,
>   He showed our feet the way;
> Up to the Lord our flesh shall fly
>   At the great rising day.

Then shall we know in the perfection of our resurrection beauty that we are indeed completely risen in Christ, and "as in Adam all die, so in Christ shall all be made alive."

This morning we shall only speak of our fellowship with Christ in His resurrection as to our own spiritual resurrection. Do not misunderstand me as if I thought the resurrection to be only spiritual, for a literal rising from the dead is yet to come; but our text speaks of spiritual resurrection, and I shall therefore endeavor to set it before you.

Our Spiritual Rising with Christ

First, then, LET US CONSIDER OUR SPIRITUAL RISING WITH CHRIST: "If ye then be risen with Christ." Though the words look like a supposition they are not meant to be so. The apostle casts no doubt, and raises no question, but merely puts it thus for argument's sake. It might just as well be read, "*Since* ye then are risen in Christ." The "if" is used logically, not theologically: by way of argument, and not by way of doubt. All who believe in Christ are risen with Christ. Let us meditate on this truth.

For, first, we were "dead in trespasses and sins," but having believed in Christ *we have been quickened by the Holy Spirit*, and we are dead no longer. There we lay in the tomb, ready to become corrupt. We lay in our death quite unable to raise ourselves therefrom; ours were eyes that could not see, and ears that could not hear; a heart that could not love; and a withered hand that could not be stretched out to give the touch of faith. We were as guilty as if we had power, for the loss of moral power is not the loss of moral responsibility: we were, therefore, in a state of spiritual death of the most fearful kind. The Holy Spirit visited us and made us live.

We remember the first sensation of life, some of us—how it seemed to tingle in our soul's veins with pain sharp and bitter; just as drowning persons when life is coming back to them suffer great pain, so did we. Conviction was wrought in us and confession of sin,a dread of judgement to come and a sense of present condemnation. But these were tokens of life, and that life gradually deepened and opened up until the eye was opened—we could see Christ, the hand ceased to be withered, and we stretched it out and touched His garment's hem; the feet began to move in the way of obedience, and the heart felt the sweet glow of love within. Then the eyes, not content with seeing, fell to weeping; and afterward when the tears were wiped away, they flashed and sparkled with delight.

Oh, believers in Jesus, you are not spiritually dead any longer; on Christ you have believed, and that grand act proves that you are no more dead. You have been quickened by God according to the working of His mighty power, which He wrought in Christ when He raised Him from the dead and set Him at His own right hand in the heavenlies. Now, beloved, you are new creatures—the produce of a second birth begotten again in Christ Jesus unto newness of life. Christ is your life; such a life as you never knew before nor could have known apart from Him. "If ye then be risen with Christ ye walk in newness of life, while the world abideth in death."

Let us advance another step: we are risen with Christ, and therefore *there has been wrought in us a wonderful change.* When the dead shall rise they will not appear as they now are. The buried seed rises from the ground, but not as a seed, for it puts forth green leaf, and bud, and stem, and gradually develops expanding flower and fruit. Even so we wear a new form, for we are renewed after the image of Him who created us in righteousness and holiness.

I ask you to consider the change which the Spirit of God has wrought in the believer: a wonderful change indeed! Before regeneration our soul was as our body will be when it dies; and we read that "it is sown in corruption." There was corruption in our mind, and it was working irresistibly toward every evil and offensive thing. In many the corruption did not appear upon the surface, but it worked within; in others it was conspicuous and fearful to look upon. How great the change! For now the power of corruption within us is broken; the new life has overcome it, for it is a living and incorruptible seed which lives and abides forever.

Corruption is upon the old nature, but it cannot touch the new, which is our true and real self. Is it not a great thing to be purged of the filthiness which would have ultimately brought us down to Tophet where the fire unquenchable burns, and the worm undying feeds upon the corrupt?

When a body is buried, we are told by the apostle again that it is "sown in weakness." The poor dead frame cannot lay itself down in its last bed, friendly hands must place it there; even so we were utter weakness toward all good. When we were the captives of sin we could do nothing good, even as our Lord said, "Without me ye can do nothing." We were incapable of even a good thought apart from Him. But "when we were yet without strength, in due time Christ died for the ungodly"; and now we know Him and the power of His resurrection. God has given us the spirit of power and of love; is it not written, "As many as received him, to them gave he power to become the sons of God, even to them that believe on his name"? This change from the natural to the spiritual is such as only God Himself could have wrought, and yet we have experienced it. To God be the glory. So that by virtue of our rising in Christ we have received life and have become the subjects of a wondrous change—"old things are passed away; behold, all things are become new."

In consequence of our receiving this life and undergoing this change *the things of the world and sun become a tomb to us.* To a dead man a sepulcher is as good a dwelling as he can want. You may call it his bedchamber, if you will; for he lies within it as unconscious as if he were in slumber. But the moment the dead man lives, he will not endure such a bedchamber; he calls it a dreary vault, a loathsome dungeon, an unbearable charnel, and he must leave it at once. So when you and I were natural men, and had no spiritual life, the things of this life contented us; but it is far otherwise now. A merely outward religion was all that we desired; a dead form suited a dead soul. Judaism pleased those who were under its yoke, in the very beginning of the gospel; new moons and holy days and traditional ordinances, and fasting and feasting were great things with those who forgot their resurrection with Christ.All those things make pretty furniture for a dead man's chamber; but when the eternal life enters the soul these outward ordinances are flung off, the living man rends off his graveclothes, and demands such garments as are suitable for life. So the apostle in the chapter before our text tells us to let no man spoil us by the traditions of men and the inventions of a dead ritualism, for these things are not the portion of renewed and spiritual men.

So, too, all merely carnal objects become as a grave to us, whether they be sinful pleasures or selfish gains. For the dead man the shroud, the coffin, and the vault are suitable enough; but make the corpse alive again, and he cannot rest in the coffin; he makes desperate struggles to break it up. See how by main force he dashes up the lid, tears off his bandages, and leaps from the bier. So the man renewed by grace cannot abide sin, it is a coffin to him: he cannot bear evil pleasures, they are as a shroud; he cries for liberty. When resurrection comes the man uplifts the hillock above the his grave, and scatters monument and headstone, if these are raised above him. Some souls are buried under a mass of self-righteousness, like wealthy souls are buried under a mass of self-righteousness, like wealthy men on whom shrines of marble have been heaped; but all these the believer shakes off, he must have them away, he cannot bear these dead works. He cannot live otherwise than by faith; all other life is death to him. He must get out of his former state; for as a tomb is not a fit place for a living man, so when we are quickened by grace the things of sin, and self, and carnal sense become dreary catacombs to us, wherein our soul feels buried, and out of which we must arise. How can we who are raised out of the death of sin live any longer therein?

And, now, beloved, *we are at this time wholly raised from the dead* in a spiritual sense. Let us think of this, for our Lord did not have His head quickened while His feet remained in the sepulcher; but He arose a perfect and entire Man, alive throughout. Even so have we been renewed in every part. We have received, though it be but in its infancy, a perfect spiritual life: we are perfect in Christ Jesus. In our inner man our eye is opened, our ear is awakened, our hand is active, our foot is nimble: our every faculty is there, though as yet immature, and needing development, and having the old dead nature to contend with.

Moreover, and best of all, we are so raised that *we shall die no more.* O tell me no more the dreary tale that a man who has received the divine life may yet lose grace and perish. With our Bible in our hands we know better. "Christ being raised from the dead dieth no more, death hath no more dominion over him," and therefore he that has received Christ's life in him shall never die. Has He not said, "He that believes in me, though he were dead yet shall he live; and whosoever liveth and believeth in me shall never die"? This life which He has given us shall be in us "a well of water, springing up unto everlasting life." He has Himself said, "I give unto my sheep eternal life, and they shall never perish, neither shall any pluck them out of my hand."

On the day of our quickening we bid farewell to spiritual death, and to the sepulcher wherein we slept under sin's dominion. Farewell, you deadly love of sin; we have done with you! Farewell, dead world, corrupt world; we have done with you! Christ has raised us. Christ has given us eternal life. We forsake forever the dreary abodes of death, and seek the heavenly places. Our Jesus lives, and because He lives we shall live also, world without end.

Thus I have tried to work out the metaphor of resurrection by which our spiritual renewal is so well set forth.

Exercising the New Life

We are urged by the apostle to use the life which we have received, and so, secondly, LET US EXERCISE THE NEW LIFE IN SUITABLE PURSUITS. "If ye then be risen with Christ, seek those things which are above." Let your actions be agreeable to your new life.

First, then, *let us leave the sepulcher.* If we are quickened, our first act should be to leave the region of death. Let us quit the vault of a merely outward religion, and let us worship God in spirit and in truth. Let us have done with priestcraft, and all the black business of spiritual undertaking, and let the dead bury their dead; we will have none of it. Let us have done with outward forms, and rites, and ceremonies which are not of Christ's ordaining, and let us know nothing save Christ crucified; for that which is not of the living Lord is a mere piece of funeral pomp fit for the cemeteries of formalists whose whole religion is a shoveling in of dust on coffin-lids. "Earth to earth, ashes to ashes, dust to dust." "That which is born of the flesh is flesh."

Let us also quit the vault of carnal enjoyments, wherein men seek to satisfy themselves with provision for the flesh. Let us not live by the sight of the eye, nor by the hearing of the ear. Let us not live for the amassing of wealth or the gaining of fame, for these ought to be as dead things to the man who is risen in Christ. Let us not live for the world which we see, nor after the fashion of men to whom this life is everything. Let us live as those who have come out of the world, and who, though they are in it, are no more of it. Let us be unmindful of the country from whence we came and leave it, as Abraham did, as though there were no such country, henceforth dwelling with our God, sojourners with Him, seeking "a city which hath foundations, whose builder and maker is God." As Jesus Christ left behind Him all the abodes of death, let us do the same.

And, then, let us *hasten to forget every evil, even as our Lord hastened to leave the tomb.* How little a time, after all, did He sojourn among the dead. He must needs lie in the heart of the earth three days, but He made them as short as possible so that it is difficult to make out the three days at all. They were there, for there were fragments of each period, but surely never were three days so short as Jesus made them. He cut them short in righteousness, and being loosed from the pains of death, He rose early at the very break of day. At the first instant that it was possible for Him to get away from the sepulcher consistently with the Scriptures He left the napkin and the graveclothes and stood in the garden, waiting to salute His disciples. So let it be with us: there should be no lingering, no loitering, no hankering after the world, no clinging to its vanities, no making provision for the flesh. Up in the morning early, from your ease, your carnal pleasure, your love of wealth and self, and away out from the dark vault into a congenial sphere of action: "If ye then be risen with Christ, seek those things which are above."

To pursue the analogy: when our Lord had left the tomb thus early He spent a season on earth among His disciples, and *we are to pass the time of our sojourning here on earth as His was passed and in holy service.* Our Lord reckoned that He was on the move from earth as soon as He rose. If you remember, He said, "I ascend unto my Father, and your Father." He did not say, "I shall ascend," as though He looked at it as a future thing; but He said, "I ascend," as if it were so quickly to be done that it was already doing. Forty days He stayed, for He had forty days' work to do; but He looked upon Himself as already going up into heaven. He had done with the world, He had done with the grave, and now He said, "I ascend to my Father, and your Father."

We also have our forty days to tarry here; the period may be longer or shorter as the providence of God ordains. But it will soon be over, and the time of our departure will come. Let us spend our risen life on earth as Jesus spent His—in a greater seclusion from the world and in greater nearness to heaven than ever. Our Lord occupied Himself much in testimony, manifesting Himself, as we have already seen, in divers ways, to His friends and followers. Let us also manifest the fruits of our risen life, and bear testimony to the power of God. Let all men see that you are risen. So live that there can be no more doubt about your spiritual resurrection than there was about Christ's literal resurrection. Let us spend the time of our sojourning here in the fear of God worshiping Him, serving Him, glorifying Him, endeavoring to set everything in order for the extension of our Master's kingdom, for the comforting of His saints, for the accomplishment of His sacred purposes.

But now I have led you up so far, I want to go further and rise higher. May the Lord help us. *Let our minds ascend to heaven in Christ.* Even while our bodies are here we are to be drawn upward with Christ—attracted to Him, so that we can say, "He hath raised us up together and made us sit together in heavenly places in Christ Jesus." Our text says, "Seek those things which are above where Christ sitteth on the right hand of God"; what is this but rising to heavenly pursuits? Jesus has gone up; let us go up with Him. As to these bodies, we cannot as yet ascend, for they are not fit to inherit the kingdom of God; yet let our thoughts and hearts mount up and build a happy rest on high. Let not a stray thought alone ascend like one lone bird which sings and mounts the sky; but let our whole mind, soul, spirit, heart, arise as when doves fly as a cloud.

Let us be practical, too, and in very deed seek the things that are above: seek them because we feel we need them; seek them because we greatly prize them; seek them because we hope to gain them, for a man will not heartily seek for that which he has no hope of obtaining. The things which are above which we are even now to seek are such as these; let us seek heavenly communion, for we are no more numbered with the congregation of the dead, but we have fellowship in Christ's resurrection and with all the risen ones. "Truly our fellowship is with the Father and with his Son Jesus Christ," and "our conversation is in heaven." Let us seek to walk with the living God, and to know the fellowship of the Spirit.

Let us seek heavenly graces; for "every good gift and ever perfect gifts is from above." Let us seek more faith, more love, more patience, more zeal: let us labor after greater charity, greater brotherly kindness, greater humbleness of spirit. Let us labor after likeness to Christ that He may be the firstborn among many brethren. Seek to bear the image of the heavenly and to wear those jewels which adorn heavenly spirits.

"Seek those things which are above," that is, heavenly joys. O seek to know on earth the peace of heaven, the rest of heaven, the victory of heaven, the service of heaven, the communion of heaven, the holiness of heaven: you may have foretastes of all these, seek after them. Seek, in a word, to be preparing for the heaven which Christ is preparing for you. You are soon to dwell above; robe yourselves for the great festival. Your treasure is above, let your hearts be with it. All that you are to possess in eternity is above where Christ is; rise, then, and enjoy it. Let hope anticipate the joys which are reserved, and so let us begin our heaven here below. If you then be risen with Christ, live according to your risen nature for your life is hid with Christ in God.

What a magnet to draw us toward heaven should this fact be—Christ sits at God's right hand. Where should the wife's thoughts be when her husband is away but with the absent and beloved one? You know, brethren, it is not otherwise with us: the objects of our affection are always followed by our thoughts. Let Jesus, then, be as a great loadstone, drawing our meditations and affections toward Himself. He is *sitting* for His work is done; as it is written, "This man, when he had offered one sacrifice for sins forever, sat down at the right hand of God." Let us rise and rest with Him. He is sitting on a throne. Observe His majesty, delight in His power, and trust in His dominion. He is sitting at the right hand of God in the place of honor and favor. This is a proof that we are beloved and favored of God, for our representative has the choicest place, at God's right hand. Let your hearts ascend and enjoy that love and favor with Him. Take wing, my thoughts, and fly away to Jesus. My soul, have you not often said, "Woe's me that I dwell in Meschech, and tabernacle in the tents of Kedar: oh that I had wings like a dove, that I might flee away and be at rest"? Now, then, my soul, here are wings for you. Jesus draws you upward. You have a right to be where Jesus is, for you are married to Him; therefore let your thoughts abide with Him, rest in Him, delight in Him, rejoice in Him, and yet again rejoice. The sacred ladder is before us; let us climb it until by faith we sit in the heavenlies with Him.

May the Spirit of God bless these words to you.

Delighting in Suitable Things

Thirdly, inasmuch as we are risen with Christ, LET THE NEW LIFE DELIGHT ITSELF IN SUITABLE OBJECTS. This brings in the second verse: "Set your affection on things above, not on things on the earth." "Set your affection." These words do not quite express the meaning, though they are as near it as any one clause could well come. We might render it thus: "Have a relish for things above"; or, "study industriously things above"; or, "set your mind on things above, not on things on the earth." That which is proper enough for a dead man is quite unsuitable for a risen one. Objects of desire which might suit us when we were sinners are not legitimate nor worthy objects for us when we are made saints. As we are quickened we must exercise life, and as we have ascended we must love higher things than those of earth.

What are these "things above" which we should set our affection upon? I ask you now to lift your eyes above yon clouds and this lower firmament to the residence of God. What see you there? First, there is *God Himself.* Make Him the subject of your thoughts, your desires, your emotions, your love. "Delight thyself also in the Lord, and he will give thee the desires of thine heart." "My soul, wait thou only upon God, for my expectation is from him." Call Him "God my exceeding joy." Let nothing come between you and your heavenly Father. What is all the world if you have not God, and when you once have God, what matters it though all the world be gone? God is all things, and when you can say "God is mine," you are richer than Croesus. O to say, "Whom have I in heaven but thee? and there is none upon earth that I desire beside thee." O to love God with all our heart, and with all our soul, and with all our mind, and with all our strength: that is what the law required, it is what the gospel enables us to render.

What see I next? I see *Jesus*, who is God, but yet is truly Man. Need I press upon you, beloved, to set your love upon the Well-beloved? Has He not won your heart, and does He not hold it now as under a mighty spell? I know you love Him. Fix your mind on Him then. Often meditate upon His divine person, His perfect work, His mediatorial glory, His second coming, His glorious reign, His love for you, your own security in Him, your union with Him. O let these sweet thoughts possess your breasts, fill your mouths, and influence your lives. Let the morning break with thoughts of Christ, and let your last thought at night be sweetened with His presence. Set your affection upon Him who has set His affection upon you.

But what do I next see above? I see *the new Jerusalem*, which is the mother of us all. I see the church of Christ triumphant in heaven with which the church militant is one. We do not often enough realize the fact that we are come unto the general assembly and church of the firstborn-whose names are written in heaven. Love all the saints, but do not forget the saints above. Have fellowship with them, for we make but one communion. Remember those—

> Who once were mourning here below,
> And wet their couch with tears,
> Who wrestled hard, as we do now,
> With sins, and doubts, and fears.

Speak with those who have won their crowns, the heroes who have fought a good fight, and now rest from their labors, waving the palm. Let your hearts be often among the perfected with whom you are to spend eternity.

And what else is there above that our hearts should love but *heaven itself*? It is the place of holiness; let us so love it that we begin to be holy here. It is the place of rest; let us so delight in it that by faith we enter into that rest. O beloved, you have vast estates which you have never seen; and methinks if I had an estate on earth which was soon to be mine I should wish to take a peep over the hedge now and then. If I could not take possession, I should like to see what I had in reversion. I would make an excuse to pass that way and say to any who were with me, "That estate is going to be mine before long." In your present poverty console yourselves with the many mansions. In your sickness delight much in the land where the inhabitants shall no more say, "I am sick." In the midst of depression of spirit comfort your heart with the prospect of unmixed felicity.

> No more fatigue, no more distress,
> Nor sin nor death shall reach the place;
> No groans to mingle with the songs
> Which warble from immortal tongues.

What! Are you bound to earth? Can you not project yourself into the future? The stream of death is narrow; cannot your imagination and your faith leap over the brook to stand on the hither shore awhile and cry, "All is mine, and mine forever." Where Jesus is there shall I be; where Jesus sits there shall I rest:

> Far from a world of grief and sin,
> With God eternally shut in?

"Set your affection on things above." O to get away at this present time from these dull cares which like a fog envelop us! Even we who are Christ's servants, and live in His court at times feel weary and droop as if His service were hard. He never means it to be a bondage, and it is our fault if we make it so. Martha's service is due, but she is not called to be *cumbered* with much serving; that is her own arrangement: let us serve abundantly, and yet sit with Mary at the Master's feet.

You who are in business, and mix with the world by the necessity of your callings, must find it difficult to keep quite clear of the down-dragging influences of this poor world. It will hamper you if it can. You are like a bird, which is always in danger when it alights on the earth. There are lime-twigs, and traps, and nets, and guns, and a poor bird is never safe except upon the wing and up aloft. Yet birds must come down to feed, and they do well to gather their meal in haste and take to their wings again. When we come down among men we must speedily be up again. When you have to mix with the world and see its sin and evil, yet take heed that you do not light on the ground without your Father: and then, as soon as ever you have picked up your barley, rise again, away, away, for this is not your rest. You are like Noah's dove flying over the waste of waters, there is no rest for the sole of your feet but on the ark with Jesus.

On this resurrection-day fence out the world, let us chase away the wild boar of the wood, and let the vines bloom and the tender grapes give forth their good smell, and let the Beloved come and walk in the garden of our souls, while we delight ourselves in Him and in His heavenly gifts. Let us not carry our burden of things below on this holy day, but let us keep it as a Sabbath unto the Lord. On the Sabbath we are no more to work with our minds than with our hands. Care and anxieties of an earthly kind defile the day of sacred rest. The essence of Sabbath-breaking lies in worry, and murmuring, and unbelief with which too many are filled. Put these away, beloved, for we are risen with Christ, and it is not meet that we should wander among the tombs. Nay, rather let us sing unto the Lord a new song and praise Him with our whole soul.

11

The Power of the Risen Savior

And Jesus came and spake unto them, saying, All power is given unto me in heaven and in earth. Go ye therefore, and teach all nations, baptizing them in the name of the Father, and of the Son, and of the Holy Ghost: teaching them to observe all things whatsoever I have commanded you: and, lo, I am with you alway, even unto the end of the world. Amen (Matthew 28:18–20).

The change from "the man of sorrows" before His crucifixion to the "Lord over all" after His resurrection is very striking. Before His passion He was well known by His disciples, and appeared only in one form, as the Son of Man, clad in the common peasant's garment without seam, woven from the top throughout; but after He had risen from the dead He was on several occasions unrecognized by those who loved Him best, and is once at least described as having appeared to certain of them "under another form." He was the same person for they saw His hands and His feet, and Thomas even handled Him, and placed his finger in the print of the nails; but yet it would seem that some gleams of His glory were at times manifested to them, a glory which had been hidden during His previous life save only when He stood on the Mount of Transfiguration.

Before His death, His appearances were to the general public—He stood in the midst of Scribes and Pharisees and publicans and sinners, and preached the glad tidings; but now He appeared only to His disciples, sometimes to one, at another time to two, on one occasion to about 500 brethren at once, but always to His disciples, and to them only. Before His death His preaching was full of parable, plain to those who had understanding, but often dark and mysterious even to His own followers, for it

* This sermon is taken from *The Metropolitan Tabernacle Pulpit* and was preached on Sunday morning, October 25, 1874.

was a judgment from the Lord upon that evil generation that seeing they should not see, and hearing they should not perceive. Yet with equal truth we may say that our Lord before His death brought down His teaching to the comprehension of the uninstructed minds which listened to it, so that many of the deeper truths were slightly touched upon because they were not able to bear them as yet.

Till His crucifixion He veiled the effulgence of many truths, but after His resurrection He spoke no more in parables, but introduced His disciples into the inner circle of the great doctrines of the kingdom, and as it were showed Himself face to face to them. Before His death the Lord Jesus was ever with His followers, and even the secret places of His retirement were known to them, but after He had risen He came and went among them at irregular intervals. Where He was during many of those forty days who among us can tell? He was seen in the garden upon Olivet, He walked to Emmaus, He comforted the assembly at Jerusalem, He showed Himself again to the disciples at the Sea of Tiberias, but where went He when, after the various interviews, He vanished out of their sight?

They were in the room alone, the doors were shut, and suddenly He stood in the midst of them; again He called to them from the sea-beach, and on landing they found a fire of coals kindled, and fish laid thereon, and bread; His appearings were strange, and His disappearings equally so. Everything betokened that after He had risen from the dead He had undergone some marvelous change, which had revealed in Him that which had been concealed before, though still His identity was indisputable.

It was no small honor to have seen our risen Lord while yet He lingered here below. What must it be to see Jesus as He is now! He is the same Jesus as when He was here; yonder memorials as of a lamb that has been slain assure us that He is the same man. Glorified in heaven His real manhood sits, and it is capable of being beheld by the eye and heard by the ear, but yet how different. Had we seen Him in His agony, we should all the more admire His glory. Dwell with your hearts very much upon Christ crucified, but indulge yourselves full often with a sight of Christ glorified. Delight to think that He is not here, for He is risen; He is not here, for He has ascended; He is not here, for He sits at the right hand of God and makes intercession for us. Let your souls travel frequently the blessed highway from the sepulcher to the throne. As in Rome there was a *Via Sacra* along which returning conquerors went from the gates of the city up to the heights of the Capitol, so is there another *Via Sacra* which you ought often to survey, for along it the risen Savior went in glorious majesty from the tomb of Joseph of Arimathea up to the eternal dignities of His Father's right hand. Your soul will do well to see her dawn of hope in His death, and her full assurance of hope in His risen life.

Today my business is to show, as far as God the Spirit may help me, first, *Our Lord's resurrection power*! and secondly, *Our Lord's mode of exercising the spiritual part of that power so far as we are concerned.*

Our Lord's Resurrections Power

Jesus said: "All power is given unto me in heaven and in earth." At the risk of repeating myself, I should like to begin this head by asking you to remember last Sabbath morning's sermon, when we went to Gethsemane and bowed our spirits in the shade of those gray olives at the sight of the bloody sweat. What a contrast between that and this! There you saw the weakness of man, the bowing, the prostrating, the crushing of the manhood of the Mediator; but here you see the strength of the God-man: He is girt with omnipotence though still on earth when He spoke these words. He had received a privilege, honor, glory, fullness, and power which lifted Him far above the sons of men. He was, as Mediator, no more a sufferer, but a sovereign; no more a victim, but a victor; no more a servant, but the monarch of earth and heaven. Yet He had never received such power if He had not endured such weakness. All power had never been given to the Mediator if all comfort had not been taken away. He stooped to conquer. The way to His throne was downward. Mounting upon steps of ivory, Solomon ascended to his throne of gold. But our Lord and Master descended that He might ascend, and went down into the awful deeps of agony unutterable that all power in heaven and earth might belong to Him as our Redeemer and Covenant Head.

Now think a moment of these words, "*All power.*" Jesus Christ has given to Him by His Father, as a consequence of His death, "all power." It is but another way of saying that the Mediator possesses omnipotence, for omnipotence is but the Latin of "all power." What mind shall conceive, what tongue shall set in order before you, the meaning of all power? We cannot grasp it; it is high, we cannot attain unto it. Such knowledge is too wonderful for us. The power of self-existence, the power of creation, the power of sustaining that which is made, the power of fashioning and destroying, the power of opening and shutting, of overthrowing or establishing, of killing and making alive, the power to pardon and to condemn, to give and to withhold, to decree and to fulfill, to be, in a word, "head over all things to his church"—all this is vested in Jesus Christ our Lord. We might as well attempt to describe infinity or map the boundless as to tell what "all power" must mean. But whatever it is, it is all *given* to our Lord, all lodged in those hands which once were fastened to the wood of shame, all left with that heart which was pierced with the spear, all placed as a crown upon that head which was surrounded with a coronet of thorns.

"All power *in heaven*" is His. Observe that! Then He has the power of God, for God is in heaven; and the power of God emanates from that central throne. Jesus, then, has divine power. Whatever Jehovah can do, Jesus can do. If it were His will to speak another world into existence, we should see tonight a fresh star adorning the brow of night. Were it His will at once to fold up creation like a worn out vesture, lo the elements would pass away, and yonder heavens would be shriveled like a scroll. The power which binds the sweet influences of the Pleiades and looses the bands of Orion is with the Nazarene; the Crucified leads forth Arcturus with his sons. Angelic bands are waiting on the wing to do the bidding of Jesus of Nazareth, and cherubim and seraphim and the four living creatures before the throne unceasingly obey Him. He who was despised and rejected of men now commands the homage of all heaven, as "God over all, blessed forever."

"All power in heaven" relates to the providential skill and might with which God rules everything in the universe. He holds the reins of all created forces, and impels or restrains them at His will, giving force to law and life to all existence. The old heathen dreamed of Apollo as driving the chariot of the sun and guiding its fiery steeds in their daily course, but it is not so: Jesus is Lord of all. He harnesses the winds to His chariot and thrusts a bit into the mouth of the tempest, doing as He wills among the armies of heaven and the inhabitants of this lower world. From Him in heaven emanates the power which sustains and governs this globe, for the Father has committed all things into His hands. "By him all things consist."

"All power" must include—and this is a practical point to us—all the power of the Holy Spirit. In the work which lies nearest our heart the Holy Spirit is the great force. It is He who convinces men of sin, and leads them to a Savior, gives them new hearts and right spirits, and plants them in the church, and then causes them to grow and become fruitful. The power of the Holy Spirit goes forth among the sons of men according to the will of our Lord. As the anointing oil poured upon Aaron's head ran down his beard, and bedewed the skirts of his garments, so the Spirit which has been granted to him without measure flows from Him to us. He has the residue of the Spirit, and according to His will the Holy Spirit goes forth into the church and from the church into the world to the accomplishment of the purposes of saving grace. It is not possible that the church should fail for want of spiritual gifts or influence while her heavenly Bridegroom has such overflowing stores of both.

All the power of the sacred Trinity, Father, Son, and Spirit, is at the command of Jesus, who is exalted far above all principality, and power, and might, and dominion, and every name that is named, not only in this world, but in that which is to come.

Our Lord also claimed that all power had been given to Him *on earth.* This is more than could be truly said by any mere man; none of mortal race may claim all power in heaven, and when they aspire to all power on earth it is but a dream. Universal monarchy has been strained after. It has seldom, if ever, been attained; and when it seemed within the clutch of ambition, it has melted away like a snowflake before the sun. Indeed, if men could rule all their fellows, yet they would not have all power on earth, for there are other forces which scorn their control. Dread diseases laugh at the power of men. The King of Israel, when Naaman came to him to be recovered of his leprosy, cried, "Am I God, to kill and to make alive, that this man doth send unto me to recover a man of his leprosy?" He had not all power. Winds and waves, moreover, scorn mortal rule. It is not true that even Britannia rules the waves. The proudest princes have been made to feel by sickness, and pain, and death that after all they were but men. Oftentimes their weaknesses have been such as to make the more apparent the truth that power belongs unto God, and unto God alone, so that when He entrusts a little of it to the sons of men, it is so little that they are fools if they boast thereof. See, then, before us a wonder. A Man who has power over all things on earth without exception and is obeyed by all creatures, great and small, because the Lord Jehovah has put all things under His feet.

For our purposes it will be most important for us to remember that our Lord has "all power" over the minds of men, both good and bad. He calls whomsoever He pleases into His fellowship, and they obey. Having called them, He is able to sanctify them to the highest point of holiness, working in them all the good pleasure of His will with power. The saints can be so influenced by our Lord through the Holy Spirit that they can be impelled to the divinest ardors, and elevated to the sublimest frames of mind. Often do I pray, and I doubt not the prayer has come from you too, that God would raise up leaders in the church—people full of faith and of the Holy Spirit, standard-bearers in the day of battle. The preachers of the gospel who preach with any power are few; still might John say, "Ye have not many fathers." More precious than the gold of Ophir are those who stand out as pillars of the Lord's house, bulwarks of the truth, champions in the camp of Israel. How few are our apostles! We want again Luthers, Calvins, Bunyans, Whitfields, men fit to mark eras, whose names breathe terror in our foemen's ears. We have dire need of such. Where are they? Whence will they come to us? We cannot tell in what farmhouse or village smithy, or school house such may be, but our Lord has them in store. They are the gifts of Jesus Christ to the church, and will come in due time. Let us believe in the power of Jesus to give us valiant men and women of renown, and we little know how soon He will supply them.

Since all power on earth is lodged in Christ's hands, He can also clothe any and all of His servants with a sacred might by which their hands shall be sufficient for them in their high calling. Without bringing them forth into the front ranks, He can make them occupy their appointed stations till He comes girt with a power which shall make them useful. Beloved, the Lord Jesus can make you eminently prosperous in the sphere in which He has placed you; my sister, your Lord can bless the little children who gather at your knee through your means. You are very feeble, and you know it; but there is no reason why you should not be strong in Him. If you look to the strong or strength, He can endue you with power from on high and say to you as to Gideon, "Go in this thy might." Your slowness of speech need not disqualify you, for He will be with your mouth as with Moses. Your want of culture need not hinder you, for Shamgar with his oxgoad smote the Philistines; and Amos, the prophet, was a herdsman.

Like Paul, your personal presence may be despised as weak, and your speech as contemptible, but yet like him you may learn to glory in infirmity, because the power of God rests upon you. You are not straitened in the Lord, but in yourselves, if straitened at all. You may be as dry as Aaron's rod, but He can make you bud and blossom, and bring forth fruit. You may be as nearly empty as the widow's curse, yet will He cause you still to overflow toward His saints. You may feel yourself to be as near sinking as Peter amid the waves, yet will He keep you from your fears. You may be as unsuccessful as the disciples who had toiled all night and taken nothing, yet He can fill your boat till it can hold no more. No one knows what the Lord can make of him, nor what He may do by him. Only this we do know assuredly that "all power" is with Him by whom we were redeemed and to whom we belong.

O, believers, resort to your Lord to receive out of His fullness grace for grace. Because of this power we believe that if Jesus willed He could stir the whole church at once to the utmost energy. Does she sleep? His voice can awaken her. Does she restrain prayer? His grace can stimulate her to devotion. Has she grown unbelieving? He can restore her ancient faith. Does she turn her back in the day of battle, troubled with skepticisms and doubts? He can restore her unwavering confidence in the gospel, and make her valiant till all her sons and daughters shall be heroes of faith and put to flight the armies of the aliens.

Let us believe, and we shall see the glory of God. Let us believe, I say, and once again our conquering days shall come when one shall chase a thousand, and two shall put ten thousand to flight. Never despair for the church; be anxious for her and turn your anxiety into prayer, but be hopeful evermore, for her Redeemer is mighty and will stir up His strength. "The Lord of Hosts is with us; the God of Jacob is our refuge." Degenerate as we are, there stands one among us whom the world sees not, whose shoe's latchet we are not worthy to unloose: He shall again baptize us with the Holy Spirit and with fire, for "all power is given unto him."

It is equally true that all power is given unto our Lord over the whole of mankind, even over that part of the race which rejects and continues in willful rebellion. He can use the ungodly for His purposes. We have it on inspired authority that Herod and Pilate, with the Gentiles and the people of Israel, were gathered together to do whatsoever the Lord's hand and counsel determined before to be done. Their utmost wickedness did but fulfill the determinate counsel of God. Thus does He make the wrath of man to praise Him, and the most rebellious wills to be subservient to His sacred purposes. Jesus' kingdom rules over all. The powers of hell and all their hosts, with the kings of the earth, and the rulers set themselves and take counsel together, and all the while their rage is working out His designs. Little do they know that they are but drudges to the King of Kings, scullions in the kitchen of His imperial palace. All things do His bidding., His will is not thwarted. His resolves are not defeated. The pleasure of the Lord prospers in His hands.

By faith I see Him ruling and overruling on land and sea, and in all deep places—guiding the decisions of parliaments, dictating to dictators, commanding princes, and ruling emperors. Let Him but arise, and they who hate Him shall flee before Him. As smoke is driven, so will He drive them away. As wax melts before the fire, so shall all His enemies perish at His presence.

As to *sinful men* in general, the Redeemer has power over their minds in a manner wonderful to contemplate. At the present moment we very much deplore the fact that the current of public thought runs strongly toward Popery, which is the alias of idolatry. Just as in Old Testament history the people of Israel were always breaking away after their idols, so is it with this nation. The Israelites were cured of their sin for a little while, so long as some great teacher or judge had power among them. But at his death they turned aside to worship the queen of heaven or the calves of Bethel, or some other visible symbols. So it is now. Men are mad after the idols of old Rome. Well, what next? Are we despairing? God forbid that we should never despond while all power is in the hand of Jesus.

A great philosopher has told us that it is absurd to suppose that prayer can have any effect upon the events of life; but God has only to visit the nation with some judgment severely felt by all and your philosopher will become as quiet as a mouse. The current of thought can readily be turned by our Lord; He can as easily manage it as the miller controls the stream which flows over his wheel or rushes past it.. The times are safe in our Redeemer's management. He is mightier than the devil, the Pope, the infidel, and the ritualist, all put together. All glory be to Him who has all power in earth and heaven.

So too, our Lord can give, and He does give to the people an inclination to hear the gospel. Never be afraid of getting a congregation when the gospel is your theme. Jesus, who gives you a consecrated tongue, will find willing ears to listen to you. At His bidding deserted sanctuaries grow crowded, and the people throng to hear the joyful sound. Ay, and He can do more than that, for He can make the Word powerful to the conversion of thousands. He can constrain the frivolous to think, the obstinately heretical to accept the truth, and those who set their faces like a flint to yield to His gracious sway. He has the key of every human heart. He opens, and no man shuts; He shuts, and no man opens. He will clothe His Word with power and subdue the nations thereby. It is ours to proclaim the gospel and to believe that no man is beyond the saving power of Jesus Christ. Doubly dyed, yea, sevenfold steeped in the scarlet dye of vice, the sinner may be cleansed; and the ringleader in vice may become a pattern of holiness. The Pharisee can be converted—was not Paul? Even priests may be saved, for did not a great multitude of the priests believe? There is no man in any conceivable position of sin who is beyond the power of Christ. He may be gone to the uttermost in sin, so as to stand on the verge of hell; but if Jesus stretches out His pierced hand, he will be plucked like a brand out of the burning.

Beloved, we have no doubts; we entertain no fears, for every moment of time is bringing on the grand display of the power of Jesus. We preach today, and some of you despise the gospel; we bring Christ before you, and you reject Him. But God will change His hand with you before long; and your despisings and your rejectings will then come to an end, for that same Jesus who went from Olivet and ascended into heaven will so come in like manner as He was seen to go up into heaven. He will descend with matchless pomp and power, and this astonished world which saw Him crucified shall see Him enthroned. In the self-same place where men dogged His heels and persecuted Him, they shall crowd around Him to pay Him homage, for He must reign and put His enemies under His feet. This same earth shall be gladdened by His triumphs which once was troubled with His griefs.

And more. You may be dead before the Lord shall come, but you will know that all power is His for at the blast of His trumpet your bodies shall rise again to stand before His terrible judgment seat. You may have resisted Him here, but you will be unable to oppose Him then; you may despise Him now, but then you must tremble before Him. "Depart ye cursed" will be to you a terrible proof that He has "all power," if you will not now accept another and a sweeter proof of it by coming unto Him who bids the laboring and heavy-laden partake of His rest. "Kiss the Son, lest he be angry, and ye perish from the way, when his wrath is kindled but a little. Blessed are all they that put their trust in him."

How He Exercises That Power

I have, secondly, by your patience, to show our LORD'S USUAL MODE OF EXERCISING HIS GREAT SPIRITUAL POWER. Beloved, the Lord Jesus might have said, "All power is given to Me in heaven and earth; take ye then your swords and slay all these My enemies who crucified Me." But He had no thoughts of revenge. He might have said, "These Jews put Me to death, therefore go straightway to the Isles and to Tarshish and preach, for these men shall never taste of My grace." But no, He expressly said, "beginning at Jerusalem," and bade His disciples first preach the Gospel to His murderers. In consequence of His having "all power" His servants were bidden to disciple all nations.

The method by which Jesus proposes to subdue all things unto Himself appears to be utterly inadequate. To teach, to make disciples, to baptize these disciples, and to instruct them further in the faith! Good Master, are these the weapons of our warfare? Are these Your battleaxe and weapons of war? Not thus do the princes of this world contemplate conquest, for they rely on monster guns, ironclads, and engines of death-doing power.

Yet what are these but proofs of their weakness? Had they all power in themselves they would not need such instruments. Only He who has all power can work His bidding by a word and dispense with all force but that of love.

Mark that *teaching and preaching are the Lord's way of displaying His power.* Today they tell us that the way to save souls is to rig out an altar with different colored silks and satins, variable according to the almanac, and to array priests in garments of divers colors and to make men wear petticoats dishonorable to their sex. With these ribbons and embroideries, joined with incense-burning, posturing, and incantations, souls are to be saved! "Not so," says the Master, but "Go ye into all the world, and preach the gospel to every creature." Preaching and teaching and baptizing the disciples are Christ's way, and priestcraft is not Christ's way. If Christ had ordained sacramental efficacy, it would succeed. But He has ordained nothing of the kind. His mandate is—All power is given unto Me in heaven and earth, go ye, therefore, disciples, baptize, and then still further instruct in the name of the Triune God.

Remember who they were who were sent on this errand. The eleven who foremost were mostly fishermen. Does the omnipotent Jesus choose fishermen to subdue the world? He does because He needs no help from them—all power is His. We must have an educated ministry they tell us. By "an educated ministry" they mean not the ministry of a man of common sense, clear head and warm heart, deep experience, and large acquaintance with human nature, but the ministry of mere classical and mathematical students, theorists, and novices, more learned in modern infidelities than in the truth of God. Our Lord, if He had wished to employ the worldly-wise, might certainly have chosen an eleven in Corinth or in Athens who would have commanded general respect for their attainments, or He could have found eleven learned rabbis near at home; but He did not want such men: their vaunted attainments were of no value in His eyes. He chose honest, hearty men who were childlike enough to learn the truth and bold enough to speak it when they knew it.

The church must get rid of her notion that she must depend on the learning of this world. Against a sound education we cannot have a word to say, especially an education in the Scriptures. But to place learned degrees in the place of the gift of the Holy Spirit, or to value the present style of so-called culture above the spiritual edification of our clergy, is to set up an idol in the house of the living God. The Lord can as well use the most illiterate as the most learned, if it pleases Him. "Go ye," He said, "ye fishermen, go ye, and teach all nations." Carnal reason's criticism on this is—a feeble method to be worked out by feebler instruments!

Now let it be noted here that the work of preaching the gospel, which is Christ's way of using His power among men, is based only upon His having that power. Hearken to some of my brethren; they say, "You must not preach the gospel to a dead sinner because the sinner has no power." Just so, but our reason for preaching to him is that all power is given unto Jesus; and He bids us preach the gospel to every creature. I tell you this, if my Lord and Master should bid me go tomorrow to Norwood cemetery and bid the dead to rise, I would do it with as much pleasure as I now preach the gospel to this congregation. I would do it for the same reason which now leads me to urge the unregenerated to repent and be converted; for I regard men as being dead in sin, and yet I tell them to live because my Master commands me do so. That I am right in thus acting is proved by the fact that while I am preaching sinners do live; blessed be His name, thousands of them have been quickened into life.

Ezekiel had to cry, "Ye dry bones, live." What a foolish thing to say! But God justified His servant in it, and an exceeding great army stood upon their feet in what was once a large charnel house. Joshua's men were bidden to blow their trumpets around Jericho—a most absurd thing to blow a trumpet to blow city walls down—but they came down for all that. Gideon's men were bidden simply to carry lamps within their pitchers, and to break their pitchers, and stand still and cry aloud, "The sword of the Lord and of Gideon"—a most ridiculous thing to hope by this means to smite the Midianites—but they were smitten, for God never sends His servants on a fool's errand. It pleases God by the foolishness of preaching to accomplish His divine purpose, not because of the power of preaching, nor the power of the preacher, nor any power in those preached to, but because "all power" is given unto Christ "in heaven and in earth"; and He chooses to work by the teaching of the Word.

Our business, then, is just this. We are to teach, or as the Greek word has it, to make disciples. Our business is, each one according to the grace given, to tell our fellow men the gospel, and to try and disciple them to Jesus. When they become disciples, our next duty is to give them the sign of discipleship by "baptizing them." That symbolic burial sets forth their death in Jesus to their former selves and their resurrection to newness of life through Him. Baptism enrolls and seals the disciples, and we must not omit or misplace it. When the disciple is enrolled, the missionary is to become the pastor, "teaching them to observe all things whatsoever I have commanded you." The disciple is admitted into the school by obeying the Savior's command as to baptism. Then he goes on to learn; and as he learns, he teaches others also. He is taught obedience, not to some things, but to all things which Christ has commanded. He is put into the church not to become a legislator or a deviser of new doctrines and ceremonies, but to believe what Christ tells him and to do what Christ bids him.

I would close this sermon very practically. The greater part of my congregation at this time consists of persons who have believed in Jesus, who have been baptized, and have been further instructed. You believe that Jesus has all power, and that He works through the teaching and preaching of the gospel; therefore, I wish to press you with a home question. How much are you doing as to teaching all nations? This charge is committed to you as well as to me. For this purpose are we sent into the world, ourselves receivers that we may be afterward distributors. How much have you distributed?

Dear brother, dear sister, to how many have you told the story of redemption by the blood of Jesus? You have been a convert now for some time: to whom have you spoken of Jesus or to whom have you written? Are you distributing as best you can the words of others if you are not capable of putting words together yourself? Do not reply, "I belong to a church which is doing much." That is not to the point. I am speaking of that which you are personally doing. Jesus did not die for us by proxy, but He bore our sins in His own body on the tree. I ask then, what are you personally doing? Are you doing anything at all? "But I cannot go for a missionary," says one. Are you sure you cannot? I have been long looking for a time when numbers of you will feel that you must go to preach the gospel abroad and will relinquish comforts and emoluments for the Lord's sake. There can be no greater honor to a church than to have many sons and daughters bearing the brunt of the battle for the Lord.

Lo, I set up a standard among you this day, let those whose hearts God has touched rally to it without delay. The heathen are perishing; they are dying by the millions without Christ, and Christ's last command to us is "Go ye, teach all nations." Are you obeying it? "I cannot go," says one, "I have a family and many ties to bind me at home." Then, I ask you, are you going as far as you can? Do you travel to the utmost length of the providential tether which has fastened you where you are? Can you say "Yes"?

Then, what are you doing to help others to go? As I was thinking over this discourse, I reflected how very little we were most of us doing toward sending the gospel abroad.

We are, as a church, doing a fair share for our heathen at home, and I rejoice at the thought of it; but how much a year do you each give to foreign missions? I wish you would put down in your pocket-book how much you give per annum for missions, and then calculate how much percent it is of your income. There let it stand—"Item: Gave to the collection last April . . .*1s*." One shilling a year toward the salvation of the world. Perhaps it will run thus—"Item: Income £5,000, annual subscription to mission £1." How does that look? I cannot read your hearts, but I could read your pocket-books and work a sum in proportion. I suggest that you do it yourselves, while I also take a look at my own expenditure. Let us all see what more can be done for the spread of the Redeemer's kingdom, for all power is with Him. When His people shall be stirred up to believe in that power and to use the simple but potent machinery of the preaching of the gospel to all nations, then God, even our own God, shall bless us and all the ends of the earth shall fear Him. Amen.

12

The Coming Resurrection

Marvel not at this: for the hour is coming, in the which all that are in the graves shall hear his voice, and shall come forth; they that have done good, unto the resurrection of life; and they that have done evil, unto the resurrection of damnation (John 5:28,29).

The doctrine of the resurrection of the dead is peculiarly a Christian belief. With natural reason, assisted by some little light lingering in tradition or borrowed from the Jews, a few philosophers spelled out the immortality of the soul. But that the body should rise again, that there should be another life for this corporeal frame, was a hope which is brought to light by the revelation of Christ Jesus. Men could not have imagined so great a wonder. They prove their powerlessness to have invented it by the fact that still, as at Athens when they hear of it for the first time, they fall to mocking. "Can these dry bones live?" is still the unbeliever's sneer.

The doctrine of the resurrection is a lamp kindled by the hand which once was pierced. It is indeed in some respects the keystone of the Christian arch. It is linked in our holy faith with the person of Jesus Christ and is one of the brightest gems in His crown. What if I call it the signet on His finger, the seal by which He has proven to a demonstration that He has the King's authority and has come forth from God? The doctrine of resurrection ought to be preached much more commonly than it is as vital to the gospel. Listen to the apostle Paul as he describes the gospel which he preached, and by which true believers were saved: "I delivered unto you," says he, "first of all that which I received, how that Christ died for our sins according to the Scriptures; and that he was buried, and that he rose again the third day according to the Scriptures."

From the resurrection of Christ, he argues that of all the dead, and insists upon it, that if Christ be not risen both their faith and his preaching were

---

* This sermon is taken from *The Metropolitan Tabernacle Pulpit* and was preached on Sunday morning, October 17, 1869.

vain. The doctrine of the resurrection in the early church was the main battleaxe and weapon of war of the preacher. Wherever the first missionaries went they made this prominent that there would be a judgment and that the dead should rise again to be judged by the Man Christ Jesus, according to their gospel. If we would honor Christ Jesus the Risen One, we must give prominence to this truth.

Moreover, the doctrine is continually blessed of God to arouse the minds of men. When we fancy that our actions are confined to this present life, we are careless of them. But when we discover that they are far-reaching and that they cast influences for good or evil athwart an eternal destiny, then we regard them more seriously. What trumpet call can be more startling, what arousing voice can be more awakening than this news to the careless sinner that there is a life hereafter, that men must stand before the judgment seat of Christ to receive for the things done in their bodies whether they be good or evil? Such doctrine I shall try to preach this morning for just such ends, for the honoring of Christ, for the awakening of the careless. God send us good speed and abundance of the desired results.

We shall first *expound the text*, and then secondly, *endeavor to learn its lessons*.

Exposition

First we shall EXPOUND THE TEXT. No exposition will be more instructive than a verbal one. We will take each word and weigh its meaning.

Observe then, first, in the text there is a forbidding to marvel. "*Marvel not at this.*" Our Savior had been speaking of two forms of life-giving which belonged to Himself as Son of Man. The first was the power to raise the dead from their graves to a renewed natural life. He proved this on one or two occasions in His lifetime: at the gates of Nain, in the chamber of the daughter of Jairus, and again at the tomb of the almost rotting Lazarus. Jesus had power when He was on earth and has power still, if so He should will it, to speak to those who have departed, and bid them return again to this mortal state and reassume the joys and sorrows and duties of life. "As the Father raiseth up the dead, and quickeneth them; even so the Son quickeneth whom he will."

After our Lord had dwelt for a moment upon that form of His life-giving prerogative, He passed on to a second display of it and testified that the time was then present when His voice was heard to the quickening of the spiritually dead. The spiritually dead—the men who are dead to holiness and dead to faith, dead to God and dead to grace; the men that lie enshrouded in the graveclothes of evil habits, rotting in the coffins of their depravity, deep down in the graves of their transgressions—these men, when Jesus speaks in the gospel, are made to live; a spiritual life is given to them. Their dead souls are raised out of their long and horrible sleep, and they are enlivened with the life of God.

Now, both of these forms of quickening are worthy to be marveled at. The resurrection of the natural man to natural life is a great wonder; who would not go a thousand miles to see such a thing performed? The raising up of the dead spirit to spiritual life, this is a greater wonder by far.

To you, beloved, the quickening of the dead is not so great a marvel as the saving of dead souls; and, indeed, the raising of a corpse from the grave is by no means so great a marvel as the raising up of a dead soul from the sleep of sin. For in the raising up of a dead body there is no opposition to the fiat of Omnipotence. God speaks, and it is done. But in the saving of a dead soul, the elements of death within are potent; and these resist the life-giving power of grace, so that regeneration is a victory as well as a creation, a complicated miracle, a glorious display both of grace and power.

Beloved, let us humbly learn one lesson from this. We are ourselves, by nature, very like the Jews. We wonder mistrustfully; we unbelievingly wonder when we see or hear of fresh displays of the greatness of our Lord Jesus Christ. So narrow are our hearts that we cannot receive His glory in its fullness. Ah, we love Him and trust Him and believe Him to be the fairest, and the greatest, and the best, and the mightiest;, but if we had a fuller view of what He can do, the probabilities are that our amazement would be mingled with no small portion of doubt. As yet we have but slender ideas of our Lord's glory and power. We hold the doctrine of His deity. We are orthodox enough, but we have not thoroughly realized the fact that He is Lord God Almighty. Does it not sometimes seem to you to be impossible that such-and-such a grievously ungodly man could be converted? But why impossible with Him who can raise the dead? Does it not seem impossible that you could ever be supported through your present trouble? But how impossible with Him who shall make the dry bones live and cause the sepulcher to disgorge?

It appears improbable at times that our corruptions should ever be cleansed away and that we should be perfect and without spot. But why so? He who is able to present tens of thousands of bodies before His throne, who long have slept in the sepulcher and moldered into dust, what can He not accomplish within His people?

O doubt no more, and let not even the greatest wonders of His love, His grace, His power, or His glory cause you to marvel unbelievingly; but rather say as each new prodigy of His divine power rises before you, "I expected this of such a one as He is. I gathered that He could achieve this, for I understood that He was able to subdue all things to Himself. I knew that He fashioned the worlds, and built the heavens, and guided the stars, and that by Him all things consist. I am not therefore astounded though I behold the greatest marvels of His powers." The first words of the text, then, urge us to faith and rebuke all unbelieving amazement.

To the second sentence I now call your attention. The coming hour. "*The hour cometh,*" says Christ. I suppose He calls it an hour to intimate how very near it is in His esteem, since we do not begin to look at the exact hour of an event when it is extremely remote. An event which will not occur for hundreds of years is at first looked for and noted by the year, and only when we are reasonably near it do men talk of the day of the month. And we are coming very near it when we look for the precise hour. Christ intimates to us that, whether we think so or not, in God's thought the day of resurrection is very near; and though it may be a thousand years off even now, yet still to God it is but one day. He would have us endeavor to think God's thought about it not reckon any time to be long, since if it be time at all it must be short and will be so regarded by us when it is past and the day has arrived. This is practical wisdom to bring close up to us that which is inevitable and to act toward it as though it were but tomorrow morning when the trump should sound, and we should be judged.

"The hour is coming," says the Savior. He here teaches us the certainty of that judgment. The hour comes; it assuredly comes. In the divine decree this is the day for which all other days were made. If it were possible that any determination of the Almighty could be changed, yet this never shall be, for "he hath appointed a day, in the which he will judge the world in righteousness by that man whom he hath ordained; whereof he hath given assurance unto all men, in that he hath raised him from the dead." "The hour cometh." Reflect on this, that most solemn hour comes every moment. Every second brings it nearer. While you have been sitting still in this house, you have been born onward toward that great event. As the pendulum of yonder clock continues unceasingly to beat like the heart of time, as morning dawn gives place to evening shade, and the seasons follow in constant cycle, we are drifted along the river of time nearer to the ocean of eternity. Born as on the wings of some mighty angel who never pauses in his matchless flight, I onward journey toward the judgment bar of God. Beloved, by that self-same flight are you also hurried on. Look to the resurrection, then as a thing that ever comes, silently drawing nearer and nearer hour by hour. Such contemplations will be of the utmost service to you.

Our Lord's words read as if the one hour of which He spoke completely drove into the shade all other events. As if the hour, the one hour, the last hour, the hour *par excellence*, the master hour, the royal hour, was of all hours the only hour that was coming that was worth mentioning as being inevitable and important. Like Aaron's rod, the judgment hour swallows up every other hour. We hear of hours that have been big with the fate of nations, hours in which the welfare of millions trembled in the balances, hours in which for peace or war the die must be cast, hours that have been called crises of history. And we are apt to think that frequently periods such as this occur in the world's history: but here is the culminating crisis of all, here is the iron hour of severity, the golden hour of truth, the clear sapphire hour of manifestations.

In that august hour there shall be proclamation made of the impartial decisions of the Lord Christ with regard to all the souls and bodies of men. O, what an hour is this which comes on apace! My dear brethren, now and then I covet the tongue of the eloquent, and now I do so that I might on such a theme as this fire your imaginations and inflame your hearts. But let me pray you assist me now for a moment; and since this hour comes, try to think it very, very near. Suppose it should come *now* while we are here assembled; suppose that even now the dead should rise, that in an instant this assembly should be melted into the infinitely greater one, and that no eye should be fixed upon the forgotten preacher, but all fixed upon the great descending Judge, sitting in majesty upon His great white throne. I pray you bethink yourselves as though the curtain were uplifted at this moment. Anticipate the sentence which will come forth to you from the throne of righteousness, consider as though at this precise moment it were pronounced upon you! O now, examine yourselves as though the testing days were come, for such an examination will be to your souls' benefit if you be saved; and they may be to your souls' arousing if you be unconverted.

But we must pass on. "Marvel not at this: the hour is coming when all that are in the graves." Notice this very carefully, "*all that are in the graves*," by which term is meant, not only all whose bodies are actually in the grave at this time, but all who ever were buried even though they may have been disinterred, and their bones may have mingled with the elements, been scattered by the winds, dissolved in the waves, or merged into vegetable forms. All who have lived and died shall certainly rise again. All! Compute then the numberless number! Count now the countless! How many lived before the deluge? It has been believed, and I think accurately, that the inhabitants of this world were more numerous at the time of the deluge than they probably are now, owing to the enormous length of human life. Men's numbers were not so terribly thinned by death as they are now.

Think if you will from the times of the deluge onward of all Adam's progeny. From Tarshish to Sinim men covered the lands. Nineveh, Babylon, Chaldea, Persia, Greece, Rome, these were vast empires of men. The Parthians, Scythians, and Tartar hordes, who shall reckon up? As for those northern swarms of Goths and Huns and Vandals, these were continually streaming as from a teeming hive in the middle ages, and Frank and Saxon and Celt multiplied in their measure. Yet these nations were but types of a numerous band of nations ever more multitudinous. Think of Ethiopia and the whole continent of Africa; remember India and Japan, and the land of the setting sun. In all lands great tribes of men have come and have gone to rest in their sepulchers. What millions upon millions must lie buried in China and Burmah! What innumerable hosts are slumbering in the land of the pyramids and the mummy pits! Every one, both great and small, embalmed of old in Egypt. Who shall compute the number?

Hear then and believe—out of all who have ever lived of woman born, not one shall be left in the tomb; all, all shall rise. I may well say as the psalmist did of another matter, "Such knowledge is too wonderful for me; it is high, I cannot attain unto it." How has God marked all these bodies; how has He tracked the form of each corporeal frame? How shall Jesus Christ be able to raise all these? I do not know. But He shall do it, for so He declared and so has God purposed. "All that are in their graves shall hear his voice." All the righteous, all the wicked, all that were engulfed in the sea, all that slumber on the lap of earth; all the great ones, all the multitudes of the sons of toil; all the wise and all the foolish, all the beloved and all the despised. There shall not be one single individual omitted.

My dear friend, it may be best for you to look at the question in a more personal light— *you* will not be forgotten. Your separated spirit shall have its appointed place and that body which once contained it shall have its watcher to guard it till by the power of God it shall be restored to your spirit again at the sounding of the last trump. You, my hearer, shall rise again. As surely as you sit here this morning, you shall stand before the once crucified Son of Man. It is not possible that you should be forgotten; you shall not be permitted to rot away into annihilation, to be left in the darkness of obscurity. You must, you shall rise, each and every one without a solitary exception. It is a wondrous truth, and yet we may not marvel at it so as to doubt it, though we may marvel at it and admire the Lord who shall bring it to pass.

Pass on. "All that are in the grave *shall hear his voice.*" Hear! Why, the ear has gone! A thousand years ago a man was buried, and his ear—there is not the slightest relic of it left—all has vanished. Shall that ear ever hear? Yes, for He that made it hear at the first wrought as great a wonder then as when He shall make it hear a second time. It needed a God to make the hearing ear of the newborn babe; it shall need no more to renew the hearing ear the second time. Yes, the ear so long lost in silence shall hear! And what shall be the sound that shall startle that newly awakened and fresh fashioned ear? It shall be the voice of the Son of God— the voice of Jesus Christ Himself.

While this teaches us the stolidity of human nature and how depraved the heart is, it also reminds us who are careless that there is no escape. If you will not hear the voice of Jesus not, you *must* hear it then. You may thrust those fingers into your ears today, but there will be no doing that in the day of the last trump; you must hear then. O that you would hear now! You must hear the summons to judgment; God grant that you may hear the summons to mercy and become obedient to it and live. "All that are in their graves *shall* hear his voice"; whoever they may have been, they shall become subject to the power of His omnipotent command, and appear before His sovereign judgment seat.

Note the next words, "*and shall come forth.*" That is to say, of course, that their bodies shall come out of the grave, out of the earth, or the water, or the air, or wherever else those bodies may be. But I think there is more than that intended by the words, "shall come forth." It seems to imply manifestation. As though all the while men were here, and when in their graves they were hidden and concealed, but as the voice of God in the thunder discovers the forests and makes the hinds to calve, so the voice of God in resurrection shall discover the secrets of men and make them to bring for th their truest self into the light to be revealed to all. The hypocrite, masked villain as he is, is not discovered now; but when the voice of Christ sounds he shall come forth in a sense that will be horrible to him. Deprived of all the ornaments of his masquerade, the vizard of his profession torn away, he shall stand before men and angels with the leprosy upon his brow an object of universal derision abhorred of God and despised of men.

Ah! dear hearers, are you ready to come forth even now? Would you be willing to have your hearts read out? Would you wear them on your sleeve for all to see? Is not there much about you that would not bear the light of the sun? How much more will it not bear the light of Him whose eyes are as a flame of fire, seeing all and testing all by trial which cannot err! Your coming forth on that day will be not only a reappearance from amidst the shadows of the sepulcher, but a coming forth into the light of heaven's truth which shall reveal you in meridian clearness.

And then the text goes on to say that they shall come forth as *those who have done good* and those who have done evil. From which we must gather the next truth, that death makes no change in man's character and that after death we must not expect improvements to occur. He who is holy is holy still, and he who is filthy is filthy still. They were, when they were put into the grave, men who had done good; they rise as men who have done good. Or they were, when they were interred, men who had done evil; they rise as those that have done evil. Expect, therefore, no place for repentance after this life, no opportunities for reformation, no further proclamations of mercy or doors of hope. It is now or never with you, remember that.

Note, again, that *only two characters rise*. For indeed there are only two characters who ever lived; and, therefore, two to bury and two to rise again—those who had done good and those who had done evil. Where were those of mingled character whose conduct was neither good nor evil, or both? There were none such. You say, do not the good do evil? May not some who are evil still do good? I answer: he that does good is a man who, having believed in Jesus Christ and received the new life, does good in his new nature and with his newborn spirit with all the intensity of this heart. As for his sins and infirmities into which by reason of his old nature he falls, these being washed away by the precious blood of Jesus are not mentioned in the day of account; and he rises up as a man who has done good—his good remembered, but the evil washed away.

As for the evil, of whom it is asserted that they may do good, we answer: so they may do good in the judgment of their fellow men and as toward their fellow mortals, but good toward God from an evil heart cannot proceed. If the fountain be defiled, every stream must be polluted also. Good is a word that may be measured according to those who use it. The evil man's good is good to you, his child, his wife, his friend; but he has no care for God, no reverence, no esteem for the great Lawgiver. Therefore, that which may be good to you may be ill to God, because done for no right motive, even perhaps done with a wrong motive, so that the man is dishonoring God while he was helping his friend. God shall judge men by their works, but there shall be but two characters, the good and the evil. This makes it solemn work for each man to know where he will be, and what has been the general tenor of his life, and what is a true verdict upon the whole of it.

There are some of you, who with all your excellences and moralities, have never done good as God measures good, for you have never thought of God to honor Him. You have never even confessed that you had dishonored Him. In fact, you have remained proudly indifferent to God's judgment of you as a sinner; and you have set yourself up as being all you should be. How shall it be possible, while you disbelieve your God, that you could do anything that can please Him? Your whole life is evil in God's sight—only evil. And as for you who fear His name, or trust you do, take heed unto your actions, I pray you, seeing that there are only those who have done good and those who have done evil. Make it clear to your conscience, make it clear to the judgment of those who watch you (though this is of less importance), and make it clear before God that your works are good, that your heart is right, because your outward conduct is conformed unto the law of God.

I shall not keep you much longer in the exposition except to notice that the mode of judging is remarkable. Those who search the Scriptures know that the mode of judging at the last day will be entirely according to works. Will men be saved then for their works? No, by no means. Salvation is in every case the work and gift of grace. But the judgment will be guided by our works. It is due to those to be judged that they should all be tried by the same rule. Now, no rule can be common to saints and sinners except the rule of their moral conduct, and by this rule shall all men be judged. If God finds not in you, my friend, any holiness of life whatever, neither will He accept you. "What," asks one, "of the dying thief then?" There was the righteousness of faith in him, and it produced all the holy acts which circumstances allowed. The very moment he believed in Christ, he avowed Christ and spoke for Christ. That one act stood as evidence of his being a friend of God, while all his sins were washed away. May God grant you grace so to confess your sins and believe in Jesus that all your transgression may be forgiven you.

There must be some evidence of your faith. Before the assembled host of men there shall be no evidence given of your faith fetched from your inward feelings, but the evidence shall be found in your outward actions. It will still be, "I was an hungered, and ye gave me meat: I was thirsty, and ye gave me drink: I was a stranger, and ye took me in: naked, and ye clothed me: I was sick, and ye visited me: I was in prison, and ye came unto me." Take heed, then, as to practical godliness, and abhor all preaching which would make sanctity of life to be a secondary thing. We are justified by faith, but not by a dead faith; the faith which justifies is that which produces holiness, and "without holiness no man shall see the Lord." See then the two classes into which men are divided, and the stern rule by which God shall judge them, and judge yourselves that you be not condemned with the wicked.

The different dooms of the two classes are mentioned in the text. One shall rise to *the resurrection of life*. This does not mean mere existence; they shall both exist, both exist forever. But "life" means, when properly understood, happiness, power, activity, privilege, capacity. In fact, it is a term so comprehensive that I should need no small time to expound all it means. There is a death in life which the ungodly shall have, but ours shall be a life in life—a true life; not existence merely, but existence in energy, existence in honor, existence in peace, existence in blessedness, existence in perfection. This is the resurrection unto life.

As for the ungodly, there is a resurrection to damnation by which their bodies and souls shall come manifestly under the condemnation of God; to use our Savior's word, shall be *damned*. O what a resurrection! And yet we cannot escape from it if we neglect the great salvation. If we could lay us down and sleep, and never wake again, O what a blessing it were for an ungodly man! If that grave could be the last of him, and like a dog he should never start again from slumber. What a blessing! But it is a blessing that is not yours and never can be. Your souls must live, and your body must live. "O fear Him, I pray you, who is able to destroy both soul and body in hell. Yea, I say unto you, fear Him."

Applications

Our time is almost spent, but I must occupy the remaining minutes in DRAWING LESSONS FROM THE TEXT.

The first is the lesson of *adoring reverence.* If it be so that all the dead shall rise at the voice of Christ, let us worship Him. What a Savior was He who bled upon the tree! How gloriously is He who was despised and rejected, not exalted! If we could even get but to see the skirts of this truth that He shall raise all the dead out of their graves, if we did but begin to perceive its grandeur of meaning, methinks we should fall at the Savior's feet as John did when he said, "I fell at his feet as dead." O what amazing power is Yours, my Lord and Master! What homage must be due to You! All hail, Immanuel! You have the keys of death and hell. My soul loves and adores You, You ever great enthroned Prince, the Wonderful, the Counselor, King of kings, and Lord of lords.

The next lesson is *consolation* for our wounded spirits concerning our departed friends. We never mourn with regard to the souls of the righteous, they are forever with the Lord. The only mourning that we permit among Christians concerns the body, which is blighted like a withered flower. When we read at funerals that famous chapter in the epistle to the Corinthians, we find in it no comfort concerning the immortal spirit, for it is not required. But we find much consolation with regard to that which is "sown in dishonor," but shall be "raised in glory." Dead men shall live; that decaying dust shall live again. Weep not as though you had cast your treasure into the sea, where you could never find it; you have only laid it by in a casket whence you shall receive it again brighter than before. You shall look again with your own eyes into those eyes which have spoken love to you so often, but which are now closed in sepulchral darkness. Your child shall see you yet again; you shall know your child. The self-same form shall rise. Your departed friend shall come back to you, and having loved his Lord as you do, you shall rejoice with him in the land where they die no more. It is but a short parting, it will be an eternal meeting. Forever with the Lord; we shall also be forever with each other. Let us comfort one another, then, with these words.

The last lesson is that of *self-examination.* If we are to rise, some to rewards and some to punishments, what shall be my position? "What shall be my position?" let each conscience ask. How do you feel, my hearers, in the prospect of rising again? Does the thought give you any gleam of joy? Does it not create a measure of alarm? If your heart trembles at the tidings, how will you bear it when the real fact is before you, and not the thought merely? What has your life been? If by that life you shall be judged, what has it been? What has been its prevailing principle up till now? Have you believed God? Do you live by faith upon the Son of God? I know you are imperfect, but are you struggling after holiness? Do you desire to honor

God? This shall rule the judgment of your life; what was its end, and aim, and bent, and object? Imperfection there has been, but has there been sincerity? Has grace, divine grace that washes sinners in the blood of Christ, proved itself to be in you by alienating you from the sins you loved and leading you to the duties that you once neglected?

I will ask you another question: If you do not feel happy at the thought of yourself, are you quite peaceful concerning the raising of all others? Are you prepared to meet before God those whom you have sinned with among men? It is a question worthy of the sinner's thought. Of what must be the terrors of men and women who will have to meet the companions of their sins! Was not this at the bottom of Dives wishing Lazarus to be sent back to the world to warn his five brethren lest they should come into the place of torment? Was not he afraid to see them there, because their recriminations would increase his misery? It will be a horrible thing for a man who has been a debauched villain to rise again and confront his victims whom his lusts dragged down to hell! How will he quail as he hears them lay their damnation at his door and curse him for his lasciviousness! O man, your sin is not dead and buried, and the sinner whom you joined hands with in iniquity shall rise to witness against you. The crime, the guilt, the punishment, and the guilty one shall alike live again; and you shall live forever in remorse to rue the day in which you thus transgressed.

Another question, if it will be terrible to many to see the dead rise again, how will they endure to see Him, the Judge Himself, and Savior? Of all men who ever lived, He is the one that you have need to be the most afraid of, because it is He whom this day you ought most to love, but whom you forget. How many times from this pulpit have I pleaded with you to yield yourselves to Jesus Christ, and how frequently have you given Him a flat denial! It may be some of you have not quite done that; but you have postponed your decision, and said, "When I have a more convenient season I will send for you." When He comes, how will you answer Him? Man, how will you answer Him? How will you excuse yourselves? You would not have Him as a Savior, but you must have Him as your Judge to pronounce your sentence. You despised His grace, but you cannot escape His wrath. If you will but look to Jesus now, you shall find salvation in that glance. But in refusing so to do you heap up for yourself wrath when that terrible but inevitable glance shall be yours, of which the prophet says, "All the kindreds of the earth shall wail because of him." O spurn Him not, then! Despise not the Crucified! I pray you trample not upon His blood, but come to Him that so when you see Him on His throne you may not be afraid.

Beloved, I might have continued to ask more questions, but I shall close with these two. One of the best ways by which to learn what will be our portion in the future is to enquire what is our portion in the present. Have you life now, I mean spiritual life—the life that grieves for sin, the life that trusts a Savior? If so, you shall certainly have the resurrection to life. On the other hand, have you condemnation now? For he who believes not is condemned already. Are you an unbeliever? Then you are condemned now, you shall suffer the resurrection to damnation. How can it be otherwise? Seek, then, that you may possess the life of God now by faith, and you shall have it forever in fruition. Escape from condemnation now, and you shall escape from damnation hereafter.

God bless you all with the abundance of His salvation, for Christ's sake. Amen.